Business
Building Blocks

Foreword

A wise mentor once challenged me by saying that if one wants to be a professional, one is committing to a lifetime as a student. Moreover, a true professional contributes the lessons learned to the benefit of the profession.

At the pinnacle of success, there are two broad categories of people. The first are those who view themselves as a reservoir amassing and holding the fruits of their success. The second are the Gareth Johns of the world who see themselves as a conduit through which to flow the lessons and benefits of success to the next generation.

I have known Gareth and Samantha Johns professionally for the better part of a decade. They built a highly successful business by being both student and conduit. There is much to be learned from their experiences.

It has been noted that "clarity is the essence of leadership." In Business Building Blocks Gareth Johns underscores his leadership by providing a clear compilation of business fundamentals to produce an effective "How-To" guide for aspiring entrepreneurs.

Even the most brilliant innovation or greatest strategy requires committed and motivated people to bring it to life. Reflecting Gareth's deep understanding of the essentials for business success, the largest section of the book is devoted to the people side of business. While not minimizing other important business basics, his forward-thinking emphasis on the human side of business is a message of note that is often overlooked by business owners.

In my years as a CEO, peer group facilitator and executive coach, I have become firmly convinced that the ability of companies to achieve sustainable growth has more to do with their ability to develop a self-perpetuating leadership infrastructure than with driving top-line revenue. Gareth's experiences give practical evidence to that belief.

Lastly, American President John Quincy Adams is quoted as saying "if your actions inspire others to dream more, learn more, do more and become more... you are a leader." I commend Business Building Blocks to you as evidence of Gareth Johns as a leader.

Hardin M. Byars
Atlanta, GA USA
June 2021

Copyright Details

For more information about the author and to download useful content in support of the theories introduced in this book, visit:
www.garethjohns.co.uk/bbb

You can order copies of this book online via Amazon.
KDP ISBN Number: 9798594131675

Book Edition 1.0 – First Published July 2021

Cover Credit - James Vigar, Recreate Design UK Ltd.

Disclaimer: The advice provided within this book worked for me during my business endeavours but remember that your interpretation of what I have written and how you deliver these theories will also impact the level of success you may gain from this book. I wish you the best but cannot take responsibility. Equally, if you are super successful from using the tools provided in this book, I promise I won't be coming for my share of your increased profits either.

Thanks

As you read this book, you will realise I believe you can achieve more when you don't work in a vacuum but leverage the skills and input of those around you. In the creation of this book, I have been no different. The feedback from my coaching clients have made this book what it is and I will be eternally grateful for their support.

- Business Computer Solutions - Martin, Jessica, Jo & Harry.
- Higher Elevation – Nash, Amy & Paul.
- Press Start – Justin, Caroline & Mark
- Brightridge – Iain

And of course, Samantha, my wife, long-time collaborator and partner in crime who has lived with, talked about and proofed this book for more than a year. Your personal decision to get and read a copy of this book will be her reward, proving that her efforts are now equally appreciated.

Table of Contents

Introduction

To help you get the best from your investment in this book, I would first like to share some background as to why I decided to write it and how you should approach using the book to give you the best chance of driving your business and personal success.

Having already told anyone who would listen and that I have a business book to write, I decided to invest the time to get my ideas down. I am very much a task-oriented person so I am good at following a step-by-step plan if laid out for me. Without structure or a guide, I tend to wander off, creating my plan as I go. This book can serve as your guide.

Having run several businesses over the last 30 years with varying levels of success, I realised that business skills can be learned in a modular fashion. The sense of achievement that completing these modules one at a time will bring, will also provide you with a sense of satisfaction driving you to complete the process. At the end of the book, I have provided a one-page view of the modules so you can colour them green as you move to high maturity.

Simon Sinek wrote a great book in 2009 called 'Start with Why', which revolutionised my leadership and frankly, my ability to tell stories that influence behaviour. Since reading his book I realised that if someone I lead (or wish to inspire with my writing) is going to act, they first need to understand why they would be better off for doing so. They need to understand the **WHY**. Taking this knowledge, I have prefixed each educational **METHOD** with a page detailing why you will be better off for getting on and doing it.

Current Position Assessment

At the start of this exercise, I would like you to assess your current maturity across all areas of your business. You will notice the business rubric has a definition for low, medium and high maturity businesses. Be honest with yourself and maybe get someone else within your company to give their honest opinion too as a double-check.

If you believe you are on the border between two scores, select the lower maturity. Tot up your scores and see which area of your business needs the most attention. You are looking for baseline data. A starting point.

Just for some clarity, throughout the book when I talk about products, that also includes when you deliver a service as a priced product.

Foundation Plan

There are six connected modular elements. What you put in this section will guide your decision making between now and when you exit your business. Some of what's in these paragraphs you will have written down before, but for most business owners, lots of it only exists in your head and even then, in your head it is often scrambled. This is your chance to clarify your thoughts into a document that can be communicated.

Modular Learning

Ultimately you will need to master all the skills in this book to gain a level of business maturity that will drive your growth, profitability and ultimately deliver your legacy. That said, you can start by focussing on whichever of the five areas (Company-Wide, People, Sales, Delivery or Finance) that you assessed as being your lowest maturity. The chances are that the area you need to focus on is the area you least want to focus on. Don't take sales from medium to high maturity because you like that area of your business if your people area score is low. Fix that first. If you don't have the discipline to work on the right things, get a mentor or coach who will hold you to the task.

You can gain access to the Business Maturity Scoring Rubric, the Foundation Plan Template and various other supporting documents to accompany this book at the following web address.

www.garethjohns.co.uk/bbb

Business Maturity Scoring Rubric

Foundation Plan	Low	Medium	High
Purpose, Vision & Mission *Why, What & How?*	☐ Your challenge is to make enough money to still be here next year. ☐ You watch your competitors every move to emulate their success. ☐ You are happy to sign up for any work that comes your way.	☐ Your reason to exist as a business is greater than just to make a profit. ☐ You have a vision, but it changes often based on external influences. ☐ Using your instincts, you decided which new work to take on.	☐ The whole team knows why the business exists. ☐ There is a solid, clear and communicated definition of where the business is heading. ☐ You know how to say no to things that detract from achieving your vision.
Core Values *Who you are and what you stand for?*	☐ You assume that your employees' core values match your own. ☐ You believe that your core values are right for your business. ☐ You make your decisions based on what feels right for you at the time.	☐ Having agreed upon a set of core values you have them printed on the wall. ☐ Core values are fully aligned to the behaviours required to achieve the company vision. ☐ Some decisions will be made based on your interpretation of the core values.	☐ Your core values are understood by everyone, driving a positive culture. ☐ All employees demonstrate their understanding of the aligned core values through their work. ☐ The core values are strictly applied and influences all your decisions.

Foundation Plan	Low	Medium	High
Growth Plan *Who you serve and where you will find them?*	☐ You believe that everyone is a potential new customer.	☐ You now realise who your best type of customer is and wish you had more of them.	☐ You have a deep knowledge of your potential customer and direct your marketing efforts towards them
	☐ Most customers learned of you via recommendations and you hope this continues.	☐ You post on social media and attend networking meetings hoping to reach your prospects.	☐ You actively connect with the influencers for the type of customers that you wish to attract.
	☐ Your offering has been built over time, based on what your customers have demanded of you.	☐ You regularly check that you can offer at least the same products as your competitors.	☐ You know that customers buy on 'difference' and you know what sets you apart from your competitors.
Medium Term Plan *Your growth and business development goals.*	☐ Business growth just happens naturally and with some luck, most years you increase your turnover.	☐ You have a minimum desired percentage growth and some months you achieve it.	☐ You have a strategic plan that will achieve your growth target and you also understand why you don't want to grow too fast.
	☐ With a continual squeeze on your profits, you do your best to get by with the team you have already.	☐ New members of your team are recruited when the existing team feel under pressure from the workload.	☐ Based on financial controls, you recruit for your expected skills demand.
	☐ With limited budgets for investments, you habitually reckon to maximise the use of your current infrastructure.	☐ You are always open to the next thing you can invest in that may make your business better.	☐ Investments are made strategically to ensure your business infrastructure accommodates your growth target.

Foundation Plan	Low	Medium	High
Long Term Plan *The ultimate exit or business transition plan.*	☐ To date, you are so busy working in your business to think about ever leaving.	☐ You have an idea of when you want to exit the business but have yet to decide how best to achieve this.	☐ You have a clear view that has been communicated with your team about how and when you will exit.
	☐ One day you hope that your business will be worth something but haven't given it much thought yet.	☐ You have dreamt up a life-changing figure you would like from your business when you ultimately exit.	☐ Your wealth needs have helped you set a calculated business exit valuation requirement.
	☐ You have some great staff and they can cope with running the business when you take a short holiday.	☐ Some of the team are starting to step up and show some initiative bringing you new ideas.	☐ Your leadership teams' skills are continually being developed to remove their dependency on you.
Wider Perspective *Helping you gain clarity, allowing better decisions.*	☐ You work hard all year, so your choice of holiday reading will be aimed to escape work rather than remind you of it.	☐ You spend perhaps a day a month working on your business. Your time is mostly operational.	☐ With a thirst for knowledge and available time, you are always looking for the chance to find things that will improve your business skills.
	☐ You don't have time to invest in gaining a wider view of your marketplace.	☐ You seek opinions of others, but if you were being honest too many of them like you and think like you. The 'Yes' men!	☐ You have a wide council of critical friends and you know how to leverage the value they bring to your decision-making process.
	☐ Everyone in your business has their processes although they are typically not written down.	☐ Although you have lots of standard processes, they are not often reviewed.	☐ You have a process to revisit and update your processes regularly ensuring they deliver as expected.

Company	Low	Medium	High
Organisational Chart *Providing clarity of responsibility.*	☐ There is just one leader and it's you. The flat structure helps you and the business feel agile and able to change as needed. ☐ New job functions are given to whoever can take them on and they do their best. ☐ When one of your team goes on leave you will step in and cover for them.	☐ You have created a structure, but the staff don't yet understand it, as somehow lots of decisions still come back to you. ☐ Job functions have been grouped logically which has driven clarity but is not yet bringing business success. ☐ Your leaders understand the role they play in developing next-generation leaders from their teams.	☐ The structure is now formal, communicated, understood and designed to deliver the company's growth goals. ☐ Each role has the main functions formally defined and the expected outcome, which is delivering against targets. ☐ For every key role in your organisation you now have trained deputies ready to step up as required.
Corporate Image *Blue or red? Ariel or Comic Sans?*	☐ Although you have a new logo it's not yet standard across everything. Your team choose their favourite font and colour when sending emails. ☐ There are no checks on the quality of output across mediums. ☐ You are happy to give your opinion on how your branding should be used but others may provide different answers.	☐ You are working to standardise your image and have informally given guidance on how to make emails more professional. ☐ Now and again you stumble into the use of your brand that is not as you would like. ☐ When you notice your branding being used incorrectly, you react with ad-hoc training to avoid a recurrence.	☐ Your branding guidelines document details your logo, font, colours and social platform identity ensuring you have standardisation. ☐ There is a process to review and maintain consistency of all brand usage. ☐ You provide training to all staff and contractors to ensure the branding guidelines are fully understood.

Company	Low	Medium	High
Product & Service Offerings *How to manage products within your sales offering.*	☐ As your business is profitable you don't look too closely at the contribution from individual offerings.	☐ When you have an issue with an existing offering you invest the time to review it fully.	☐ There is an effective process to review all offerings for profitability, viability and risk.
	☐ There is very little time for training, so staff are expected to learn on the job.	☐ Training is put in place when there have been issues in the delivery of your offering.	☐ You assess the skills required and create training plans for all offerings.
	☐ When a customer asks for something that you don't normally sell, you find a way to supply it.	☐ You react to your competitor's innovations by imitation, wanting to have the same offerings.	☐ There is a formal process to evaluate any new solutions before they are added to your standard offerings.
Next Big Thing *Be ready for your market to be disrupted.*	☐ There still seems to be customers out there who want your products so you presume that everything is good.	☐ You have become aware what you sell today has been commoditised and has a reducing profit margin.	☐ You know where each of your offerings is in their lifecycle and are ready to transition to more profitable solutions.
	☐ You are comfortable with the products you sell and are not looking to change anytime soon.	☐ New products are being sold in your marketplace, but you don't know how or when you should begin to offer them.	☐ You keep up to date with your industry influencers and can foresee what's next for your sector before your competitors.
	☐ You are sure that what you do today will continue forever, so do not feel the need to create a budget.	☐ When new opportunities come your way, you do your best to take them and find a way to add these to your budget.	☐ You have an investment budget to ensure you are ready to sell what will ensure your business remains relevant.

Company	Low	Medium	High
Employee Wellbeing *Happier employees create happier customers.*	☐ Nobody in your organisation has any issues with their mental health as far as you know, so this is not a discussion point.	☐ When you become aware of an employee having issues you do your best to support them in any way possible.	☐ You and your leaders have a process to ensure you know what's important to each of your employees and their state of mental health.
	☐ You have a small budget to spend on your office, so you typically make do and mend whenever possible.	☐ If an employee asks for something to improve their work environment you would consider making a purchase.	☐ Working conditions are actively maintained to create the most conducive environment.
	☐ Some of the team occasionally have a night out together.	☐ You arrange a Christmas meal as a thank you to the staff.	☐ You have created a budget and support the planning of regular fun and engaging team activities.
Communication *The WHY and WHAT of effective communication.*	☐ You like to talk to people so reckon to share any important messages in person.	☐ You are known for sending verbose emails to your team, although you sometimes feel they are ignored.	☐ All your communications are succinct and drive positive outcomes.
	☐ You have plenty to do today, so don't look to second guess the communications of any employees.	☐ When a communication training need is identified, ad hoc support is given.	☐ As part of your onboarding and ongoing training employees learn how to effectively communicate.
	☐ As far as you know, your team communications does not need improvement.	☐ You typically look at your communications as part of a review of a wider business improvement.	☐ You have a culture of continual improvement that includes reviewing the effectiveness of all communications.

Company	Low	Medium	High
Risk *Planning for the unthinkable.*	☐ Risk kind of scares you so you try not to think about it too much.	☐ You have started to understand risks, but only deal with issues as they occur.	☐ Regularly, your leadership team review and update a register of all potential risks.
	☐ You recognise a risk to your business when it causes you an impact.	☐ Some of your team are good at spotting risks, but their views are rarely shared.	☐ Plans to mitigate risks is a regular team meeting item reinforcing this as a company-wide issue.
	☐ Risks are considered in isolation as bumps in the road. Once resolved, they are never given another thought.	☐ The benefits of resolving a risk are considered a bonus outcome rather than a reason to resolve the risk.	☐ The whole team understand that removing any current risks can create future opportunities and strengths.
Community *The benefits of your role in the wider community.*	☐ You are too busy worrying about what you need to do inside your business to give much thought to the wider world.	☐ Your investment in the community tends to be reactive rather than any kind of strategic alignment.	☐ You understand that community support has a positive impact on your employee and customer groups.
	☐ You don't have a budget put aside for community engagement.	☐ In an ad hoc way you choose to support events when asked by your customers.	☐ You have a defined budget to spend within your community.
	☐ You sponsor a few things but don't gain any meaningful business exposure.	☐ You have never checked that the community events you support are attended by your avatar customer.	☐ You have a strategy to engage effectively and maximise any opportunities.

People	Low	Medium	High
Leadership *Creating a culture of ownership.*	☐ Most decisions pass across your desk. The speed at which you can grow is restricted by your workload.	☐ You have come to realise that you achieve more by having great leaders to work with, who can take over some of your tasks.	☐ Your leadership team all understand that the future success of the business will come from building next-generation leaders.
	☐ Generally, your employees are happy to do what you tell them to do, without giving too much resistance.	☐ Notionally you have people called leaders, although there is not a clear definition as to what decisions they are permitted to make.	☐ All employees understand what is expected of them and what decisions they can make without seeking permission.
	☐ Owning all business decisions, you assume that this level of control is the only way to achieve success.	☐ Leaders focus solely on their departments whilst assuming you oversee the bigger picture of your business success.	☐ Leadership work together to deliver against the strategic company vision ensuring all departments function in accord.
Effective Meetings *Structures that drive performance.*	☐ Meetings only happen reactively to an external event that dictates the need to meet.	☐ Sometimes the scheduled meetings are cancelled when something else needs attention.	☐ There is a regular pulse of leadership meetings, with each one always running to time.
	☐ The agenda for your meetings are typically only to deal with the current challenge.	☐ Your agenda is rarely adhered to and often meetings go off-topic and overrun.	☐ The structured meeting agenda complete with expected timings, is followed strictly.
	☐ It's not unusual for a meeting to conclude without clarity of the root cause of the issue or how to avoid recurrences.	☐ Everyone in attendance takes their notes and leaves with their personal view of the next steps they need to perform.	☐ One set of outcomes are created which are always clear, have ownership and drive companywide actions.

People	Low	Medium	High
Shining Stars *Defining expected behaviours.*	☐ You know that some people are simply better team players, you just have never tried to work out why.	☐ Leaders have their view of what they expect from their teams but nothing is documented.	☐ There is a clear definition of what great behaviour looks like across your business so you can achieve your mission.
	☐ You are willing to tolerate some poor behaviour if in general, your employees get the job done.	☐ You have some star performers and wish you could clone them.	☐ Every leader measures the behaviours of their team against the defined standard.
	☐ The employees do not know what is expected of them to be a model employee, nor do they know how well their behaviour measures up to this.	☐ Having defined a model of expected behaviours, you don't discuss it with the employees so they still don't know how they are doing.	☐ Everyone in the company knows what the behaviour of the 'Shining Star' looks like and what they need to do extra to measure up to this model of behaviour.
Holistic One-to-Ones *The benefit of more regular check-ins.*	☐ Individual staff meetings are seen by you and your employees as a poor use of time.	☐ You and your leaders see value in meeting regularly, but the employees don't yet see the value.	☐ All leaders understand that being aligned with their team members delivers the best outcomes.
	☐ Your meeting is primarily as an irregular catch up, with the employee wanting to talk about pay rises.	☐ The agenda you create is based on recent behaviour and anything else you need to tell your employee.	☐ You have a structured agenda allowing the employee to both give and receive feedback with clear next steps.
	☐ You believe that unless an employee reaches out to you, you should focus on urgent matters.	☐ You have great intentions to regularly meet, but other things tend to get in the way.	☐ All leaders have a regular weekly check-in with their direct reports as an immovable priority.

People	Low	Medium	High
Pay Structure *How to be fair and equitable.*	☐ You pay as little as you can to get someone, so there is a large difference between your highest and lowest paid employees. ☐ Basic pay and performance have no connection, partially because you don't know what to measure. ☐ Pay increases are either because an employee threatens to leave, or because the government increased the living wage.	☐ Some areas of your business have structured pay, but you are willing to override it to retain the talent of the employee. ☐ On an annual basis you may pay a performance bonus to the people you like based on your opinions alone. ☐ Employees know that to get a pay rise they need to demonstrate their progression, but it is driven by the employee.	☐ All employees believe that the pay structure is fair and rewards those that help the company achieve its mission. ☐ All employees receive a combination of basic pay plus a bonus based on their performance. ☐ Every employee has clarity of what they can do in their role to increase their pay and is actively encouraged to achieve.
Profit-Sharing *How to keep the wantrepreneurs motivated.*	☐ You believe that everyone is paid already and profits are for owners only. ☐ If you had a good year, you may choose to buy the team lunch one day or put biscuits in the break room. ☐ Your company's performance is very much kept secret. You don't tell the employees how the finances work for fear they would worry or ask for pay rises.	☐ To keep the leadership team motivated you now pass on some of the annual profit. ☐ You decide how much profit to give your leadership team based on what you think will motivate them. ☐ You share some high-level figures but only with your leadership team. You are not ready to explain how owners are paid related to their work role and risk.	☐ As part of the company culture everyone receives a share of the company's profits. ☐ At least 10% of the company annual profits are shared across all the employees. ☐ Employees understand the economics of the business so they know how their efforts contribute to the business success and company mission.

People	Low	Medium	High
Recruitment *Hiring well today with an eye on the future.*	☐ You sift the CVs looking for a great match for your job vacancy. The interview is only used to check you like the person enough to give them a try.	☐ You have a favourite script of questions to ask at every interview, but conversations often go off track. Hires are often made on your gut feeling.	☐ With a defined job specification, and a structured multi-stage process, your interview includes core value questions and role-based exercises.
	☐ You have never considered having candidates attend work trials as part of offering them the job role.	☐ You would like to offer work trials to check that a candidate can do the job role, but often your hiring need dictates you don't have time for this stage.	☐ Your leadership team see the benefit of always bringing new employees into the company via a work trial looking to see how they act around their new colleagues to ensure culture is retained.
	☐ You don't have an onboarding plan, but new employees shadow existing team members until they can work on their own without supervision. Many recruits fail to stay past their probation period.	☐ The employee onboarding process is not formal or consistent. Because you are not monitoring the progress of their onboarding, often the wrong people stay past probation.	☐ Before your new employee starts work, you prepare fully for their arrival. Your detailed onboarding and training plans ensure that you have a very low staff turnover.

Sales	Low	Medium	High
Lead Generation *How to fill your sales pipeline.*	☐ You have some old marketing lists collected over the years that you think are your prospects. ☐ New customers mostly come by referral and although that has gone quiet of late, you are hopeful that one day you will get some new referrals. ☐ You have a legacy website but updating it isn't seen as your priority at this time.	☐ You know who you want to work with but don't have a formal list yet. ☐ You tend to ramp up your lead generation activity when you are quiet and stop again when you have work. This feast and famine are all you have known. ☐ You create a few blogs when it's quiet, but you are not sure if they are ever read.	☐ You know your prospects and have permission to contact them with your messaging. ☐ You have a repeatable process for creating new leads and know what you need to do to slow or speed that process based on your business mission needs. ☐ You measure the success of your physical, social media and people networking pillars.
New Business Process *Honing a repeatable sales methodology.*	☐ Any lead is a good lead and with excitement, you arrange to meet them without any additional research. ☐ With no formal process to assess the needs of your prospect, your first meeting is used to pitch your ideas for what you think they want from you. ☐ If a customer gives you a review on Google it's always a bonus.	☐ Before arranging to visit you have an informal chat with the prospect to check you are not wasting your time. ☐ You deliver your regular presentation at all first meetings hoping it resonates with the prospect. This is very much about what you want to sell them. ☐ You have a process to ask a customer to leave you a review after you complete your work.	☐ Only new leads that qualify against your definition of an avatar customer will progress to a first meeting. ☐ Your first meeting with a prospect is all about them. You learn all you can and then in the second meeting talk directly to the pain they have previously revealed. ☐ Reviews and testimonials are actively offered and new ones collected as part of your new business process.

Sales	Low	Medium	High
Pre-Sales Process *Why pre-planning drives project performance.*	☐ You tend to use your experience to create proposals worrying about how you will deliver later. ☐ You typically know what your customer needs, so you don't waste time second-guessing yourself. ☐ Getting to the end of the project and getting paid means you did well.	☐ You have standard templates to help your team provide proposals, albeit not ideal for bespoke projects. ☐ You check the customer's needs but often are required to sell extra things to complete the project. ☐ Reviewing your completed projects, reveals that some ran over budget.	☐ Proposals factor the labour types required and details of all materials required avoiding ordering errors. ☐ The pre-sales process ensures sales orders are delivered accurately, fulfilling the customer's needs. ☐ Your projects consistently come in on time and within budget.
Proposals *Components of a winning proposal.*	☐ You can create a brief proposal in a few minutes based on your knowledge of their needs. ☐ Your proposals are not very detailed and you believe that your customers are just after the best price. ☐ You have clear simple pricing. Typically, you don't break materials and labour down to avoid being price compared.	☐ You have a standard template to make it easy and quick for your team to create proposals. ☐ You provide a brief scope of works to justify your proposal costs. ☐ You break down materials from labour, but typically quote hourly rates rather than project costs based on the value delivered.	☐ You provide a succinct needs précis and how your proposal will address these. ☐ Your scope of works includes not only what you plan to do but also what is not included within the project. ☐ Your proposal details the materials and total labour. You offer options on your proposal to create incremental sales.

Sales	Low	Medium	High
Account Management *Investing in your customer relationships.*	☐ If a customer calls, you respond to their needs but have no formal account managers or process. ☐ You don't measure customer satisfaction and are typically unaware of any customer satisfaction issues. ☐ You hope that your customers will come to you when they next need you, so you can submit a proposal.	☐ You have an account manager, who is left to pick which clients they want to contact and how often. ☐ There are limited opportunities to build relationships, so customer satisfaction is hard to improve. ☐ As your orders pipeline dries up, you go to see your best customers, to try and get some new project orders.	☐ With a finite number of accounts to manage, your account managers consistently deliver a proven process. ☐ Your account managers build relationships, creating great customer satisfaction. ☐ You understand the client's strategic needs and help them set budgets for future spending.
Pricing Strategy *How to be profitable every time.*	☐ You have always worked on ensuring your sell everything for more than you paid for it. ☐ You sell what you think your customer will buy so don't have a formal product catalogue to sell from. ☐ You have a pricing strategy that is different for each customer, making regular universal increases difficult.	☐ You only review your pricing when you learn that your gross margin is too low. ☐ You have a standard catalogue of products but it is confused by cheaper products that you would rather not sell. ☐ You tend to defer putting up your standard prices for fear of upsetting your loyal customers.	☐ For each of your product lines you know what it costs including labour to deliver. ☐ You have a standard and a premium version of your products, knowing that about a fifth of your customers will happily pay for the premium version. ☐ Within your business terms you allow for all your selling prices to increase annually by at least inflation.

Delivery	Low	Medium	High
Project Management *Why ownership makes the difference.*	☐ Your projects are owned by whoever is delivering the project without leadership oversight or process.	☐ For bigger projects, you have a process to follow but any available member of the team could take responsibility.	☐ You have a named resource within your team responsible for project delivery against a regular process.
	☐ You don't feel you can justify charging for providing a project management service.	☐ If you think a project will require extra attention you sometimes add extra labour to cover this cost.	☐ As Project Management drives business outcome success, you always charge for this service.
	☐ You don't think too much about asking for feedback or testimonials as part of project delivery.	☐ When you are proud of how well the project was completed you sometimes ask for feedback and a testimonial.	☐ You explain at the start of the project that within your process you will always ask for feedback and a testimonial.
Measurement *What you measure, you can manage.*	☐ You consider busy employees to be productive employees, but there is nothing measured.	☐ Some of the team have targets for productivity, although these are not mapped to the business mission.	☐ You understand that measuring the right things creates the right employee behaviours and delivers results.
	☐ You don't measure activities or performance of employees unless you are looking to sack one of them.	☐ You are very interested in the activities of your employees but don't measure the outcomes.	☐ You are not interested in how much work was completed, but the results that the work has achieved.
	☐ As you don't measure much, there is a limited correlation between what you measure and strategy.	☐ The leadership are often distracted by individual's metrics when making strategic decisions.	☐ Aggregated metrics rather than individual's metrics are used by leadership to keep a focus on the company vision.

Delivery	Low	Medium	High
Root Cause Analysis *Fix it first, but then find out why it broke.*	☐ Every day has new challenges and resolving them is part of how you run your business.	☐ When something doesn't go quite right, you fix it but it frustrates you as it causes you lost time or money.	☐ You fix your challenges but also document them as an essential part of business process improvement.
	☐ Once you have dealt with a business challenge, you are on to the next challenge.	☐ When the loss of time or money was great enough, you invest some time to investigate the cause of the issue.	☐ Your process to review all previous workarounds, helps you see if you need to optimise your processes.
	☐ You consider it to be part of your role to be the main problem solver for your company.	☐ The leadership team tend to be the only people with a focus on business improvement.	☐ Positive changes to processes are shared with the team encouraging them to highlight other workarounds.
Customer Satisfaction *Knowing why your customers love or loath you.*	☐ An absence of complaints leads you to believe your customers are satisfied.	☐ Occasionally you ask customers for their feedback on the service you provide.	☐ You have a mechanism to collect regular feedback from all your customers.
	☐ Most of the complaints you receive are from customers that don't understand.	☐ When you receive a complaint, your task is to find out who to blame.	☐ You are pleased to acknowledge and act on both positive and negative customer feedback.
	☐ As you don't request customer satisfaction data, you don't have anything to help improve customer satisfaction.	☐ From the limited data you have collected, it is hard to be conclusive about what steps you need to take to create service improvements.	☐ You use the data collected to train your team to do more of what makes customers happy and less of what makes them unhappy.

Finance	Low	Medium	High
Budget *Why effective budgeting drives success.*	☐ You have some idea of what you hope to achieve but would consider creating a formal budget only if asked by a lender.	☐ You create your high-level budget for the year ahead including your ambitious growth targets.	☐ You have a detailed annual and achievable budget split into the functional areas of your business.
	☐ With an absence of a formal budget, you don't have cause to discuss this with any of your employees.	☐ The budget document is never shared with the team as it includes sensitive owner remuneration detail.	☐ The leadership team have a great working knowledge of the budget and a high-level view is shared with the whole team.
	☐ You only know how you achieved when your accounts for the year are compiled.	☐ You review the budget at the end of the year and can see the variance, but too late to impact any change.	☐ The monthly variance creates changes in the decisions being made by the leadership team.
Credit Terms *You are not a bank. Does the customer know that?*	☐ You prioritise getting and doing work. You don't feel you can influence the credit demanded. You are always owed lots of money.	☐ Although you prefer customers to pay by direct debit, you don't insist on it. Some customers still dictate their credit terms.	☐ All customers pay for everything you supply by direct debit within a fixed timescale and some services are even paid for in advance.
	☐ You look at your aged debt total like available money, so don't typically worry about debtors.	☐ Customers with poor payment history resist paying by direct debit. You continue to allow this exposure.	☐ You have a low level of bad debt. If a direct debit is cancelled you know to limit your future exposure.
	☐ You don't understand debtor days, why it matters or what you could do to impact this number.	☐ Although you know how to measure debtor days, there is no leadership focus on reducing it.	☐ You run at less than 30 debtor days consistently and it is a key leadership metric.

Finance	Low	Medium	High
Financial Control *What pays your wages?*	☐ You know which customers generate the greatest revenue, but don't worry about profitability at a per-customer level.	☐ You know that some of your customers are not very profitable, after you factor all costs, but have not created a process to resolve this.	☐ You have a regular process to proactively identify and resolve issues with customers who are out of bounds for your profit requirements.
	☐ You only look at the profitability of individual products when you first create them.	☐ When a supplier increases their component costs, you sometimes review the profit of your product.	☐ You regularly identify products that do not deliver the expected profit so you can adjust as required.
	☐ You only look closer at your fixed business costs when your sales figures are down and you are having cash flow concerns.	☐ When you review your budget, general expenses will gain more focus, but perhaps not yet actively managed.	☐ Your fixed cost business expenses are regularly reviewed and opportunities to optimise or reduce costs considered.

You have now completed the rubric section of the book. Review your scoring to see which area of your business is going to be requiring your attention as you strive to become high maturity in all areas of your business.

Foundation Plan

In short, any journey where you choose where to start and the route you decide to follow can have a massive impact on where and when you finish. In business, the stakes are high enough that it's worth putting some thinking into where you are heading and how you are going to get there.

The Business Building Blocks Foundation Plan consists of six main components which are all discussed in greater detail in the following chapters.

1. Purpose, Vision & Mission
2. Core Values
3. Growth Plan
4. Medium Term Plan
5. Long Term Plan
6. Wider Perspective

Often when people first arrive at my book, they have a current business pain to solve that is distracting them from any kind of progress they could be making with their business. If you have now worked through the 'Business Maturity Scoring Rubric' exercise you will be aware of just how much work is ahead of you to have a complete process-driven mature business.

The difference between average and amazing business success is often anchored in the attitudes of business owners around time management. We are all busy people, but it transpires that I am not too busy to write this book. A decision I actively made to get the thoughts from my head and down into a book manuscript. That decision was that I could allocate some of my time to making this book a reality. We all have 168 hours a week at our disposal. Although you are pulled around by external forces, a lot of that time is yours to invest to reach your definition of success. Your goals.

The process of documenting the Foundation Plan as your very next step will serve you because it will help you gain clarity of who you are and what you stand for. It will also help you understand how aligned your staff are, where you are going to get your next customers and who those customers are, how many new customers you need to get. Finally, this will help you with your plan and timing to move on.

Once you have this one-page document, you will be able to use it to test out your new ideas. The question "Will what I plan to do now help me reach my goal?" is easier to ask and this document will provide the answer. No more rabbit holes. No more chasing shiny things!

There is a chance that this will be the first time you have run through this type of thinking and I recommend you allow your brain to do the work. Make some notes, take a break and come back to review what you believe before you consider introducing any of this to your teams. Lastly, when it comes to long term plans ensure you work with any significant others in your life as it's great if your idea of the future has good alignment with theirs.

Foundation Plan

Creating and maintaining a one page view of your business objectives will inform your future decision making process and improve communication within your leadership team.

Business Building Blocks

Purpose, Vision & Mission

Purpose:

Vision:

Mission:

Core Values

1

2

3

4

5

Growth Plan

Avatar - Sector:
Avatar - Size:
Avatar - Geography:
List Building:
Unique:
Guarantee:
Personas:
Communication Strategy:

Medium Term Plan

Future Date:
The Future:
Turnover and Net Profit Target:
Headline Goals:

Long Term Plan

Timeline:
Current Business Valuation:
Target Business Valuation:
Exit Options:
Headline Goals:

Wider Perspective

Headline Goals (for Gaining a Wider Perspective):

Foundation Plan - Purpose, Vision & Mission

The Why?

You may not have thought about why your company exists for a long time. What difference do you make because you exist? This process will help you to imagine if you were successful, what it would look and feel like.

The advantage of having a documented Purpose, Vision and Mission will be that you can test your future tough business decisions against these statements. Put simply, if the thing you are considering doing is not going to help you achieve, it will get in the way of your achieving.

Often these three elements are introduced at the same time and consequently, their reason for consideration becomes blurred. For clarity, here is a summary of the difference between the three.

The PURPOSE statement answers WHY we exist.

Push the boundaries of our space knowledge.

The VISION statement answers WHAT we aim to achieve.

We are going to land on Mars in the next 5 years.

The MISSION statement answers HOW we plan to achieve our vision.

We are training the best astronauts and building a new rocket.

And a real-world example comes from Uber. Their statements are defined as:

Purpose: Evolve the way the world moves.
Vision: Acquire a 40% market share for paid rides in key US metropolitan markets.
Mission: By seamlessly connecting riders through our apps, we make cities more accessible, opening up more possibilities and more business for drivers.

In the next chapter, you will work on defining your business Core Values, which will very much be informed by looking for the values that will drive the behaviours you need to complete your mission that delivers against your vision, allowing you to serve your purpose.

Method

Although the task here is to create three statements, they are interlinked so you can deal with them as part of the same business building block.

Purpose Statement
1. Think about why the company was started in the first place.
2. This inspirational statement helps you explain why you exist and may not ever be achievable but will indicate a clear direction.
3. An emotional connection will come from this statement for the reader and remember, that the reader could be potential customers or employees.
4. The best-written purpose statements are about people rather than process and encourage teamwork, so are greater than any individual's contribution.

Examples
- *To create one of the most special memories in a person's life. (Disney)*
- *To solve unsolved problems innovatively. (3M)*

Vision Statement
1. Think of this as where you are planning to get to in the future. Your destination.
2. It should be one big single, future-focused and challenging vision.
3. Keep it clear and concise. Your team need to be able to commit this to memory and understand what it means. This isn't the place to use clever words.
4. Make this inspirational too, so that everyone in your organisation will want to get behind your vision but equally make it something solid that won't be impacted by market forces.
5. The vision should have a timeframe and be measurable. You should be able to report on your progress towards achieving your vision.
6. Will the Vision you have created 'guide you' for the next 3-5 years?

Examples
- *Become a $125 billion company by the year 2000. (Walmart)*
- *A computer on every desk and in every home; all running Microsoft software. (Microsoft)*

Mission Statement
1. This is the journey detailing how you will be reaching your destination.
2. To achieve your vision, will you need to create new offerings or serve new or underserved markets. Will you be creating differentiating initiatives? What makes you different?
3. Ensure this statement ties back to your vision.

Examples
- *To organise the world's information and make it universally accessible and useful. (Google)*
- *To give people the power to share and make the world more open and connected. (Facebook)*

When you have these three statements written, take a step back and reflect. Test them on your team members and see if they make sense and inspire them too. Once you have them agreed, ensure you keep them alive by mapping out the path to your vision so the team can see and help you achieve the steps required.

One final note here, it's important to keep these statements both current and relevant. Once you reach Mars, you will need to redraft your statements as you recast your vision and the mission to achieve it.

It's quite normal that your Purpose statement may remain current for much longer but again, still plan to review this periodically as part of this process.

Foundation Plan - Core Values

The Why?

When I am told by new coaching clients that they don't have any values, I take that to mean that they have them, but they have just never thought much about them or written them down.

The Core Values of the business will guide the required behaviours of everyone in the business, so this section of the book is about trying to work out what your values are so you can then start to use them purposely within the business to guide your decision making.

Avoid Aspirational Values – These are the type of values that you wish you had but are too far out of reach to be made the norm at this time.

Avoid Permission to Play Values – These are the minimum you need anyway. For example, if you are in financial services, having 'trustworthy' as a Core Value won't benefit you. This type of value doesn't serve to create the behaviours in your business that you need for success.

You may find that the Core Values of your business are very much aligned with the values of the founders. This is the DNA of any business. If the Managing Director is unwilling to invest in their learning, it is unlikely that education is one of the company's Core Values.

Getting Core Values to stick with your teams requires you to find ways to regularly discuss them. This also helps if you don't have too many. Everyone in the company should be able to recite the values and know what they mean too.

Later in the book, I will also explain how you should consider updating your interview process to create questions that will give you answers that will help you understand if a candidate is aligned to your Core Values.

Method

Stage One

Think about a few of your team who embody what you believe your company is all about. Those that deliver the behaviour you ideally want from everyone on the team if you could just clone those shining stars. It's worth asking your leadership team for their suggestions for the top three to ensure there is agreement at this stage.

Rod	Jane	Freddy

Stage Two

Think about your stars and create a list of why you have put them on the list. Don't worry if it's a long list at this stage.

Stage Three

You now need to narrow the list down. Cross through anything that is perhaps not important and remove any that are similar.

Stage Four

Pick the values common across all three of your stars.

Stage Five

You can now document each of the Core Values in a way that will ensure ambiguity never creeps into your use of these within the business. By documenting the behaviours, we get to check the understanding of the stated core value.

Core Value:	Integrity
Definition:	Doing the right thing, no matter who (if anyone) is watching
Behaviours:	Always tell the truth. Treat all people with equal value. Be ethical in all things.

Stage Six

Before you announce your newly discovered Core Values, with the help of your leadership team, review the rest of the employees against these Core Values behaviours. Mark them as being in alignment to your definition of a shining star (+), showing some alignment but needing some of your attention to bring into alignment (+/-) or potentially people who need to be helped to find another job role in another company that would be more suited to their values (-).

	Value 1 Integrity	Value 2	Value 3	Value 4
Rod	+			
Jane	+			
Freddy	+			
Mary	+			
Mungo	-			
Midge	+/-			

Stage Seven

Live with everything you have discovered for at least 3-weeks before you share details with your wider team. Watch how people work, keeping these values in your mind, so you can double-check that your marking was reasoned and fair.

Stage Eight

This is where you take the team on a journey to explain why these Core Values exist and how you are going to use them to inform your actions including how you will recruit new colleagues and customers.

From experience, this is best introduced at the team meeting and reinforced with regular discussions and activities. Team members who need individual assistance with gaining alignment will be helped as part of the regular weekly appraisal process.

My previous business held three core values, which were:

Integrity – Doing the right thing, no matter who is watching.
Dependability – Tell people what you plan to do and then do it. Every time.
Education – A quest for knowledge and supporting colleague's development.

Once you have clarity of your Core Values, here are a couple of ideas you could consider that will help your team understand and live their core values every day.

1. Awards

Give a monthly award for the member of the team who has best-demonstrated behaviours in alignment with the Core Value.

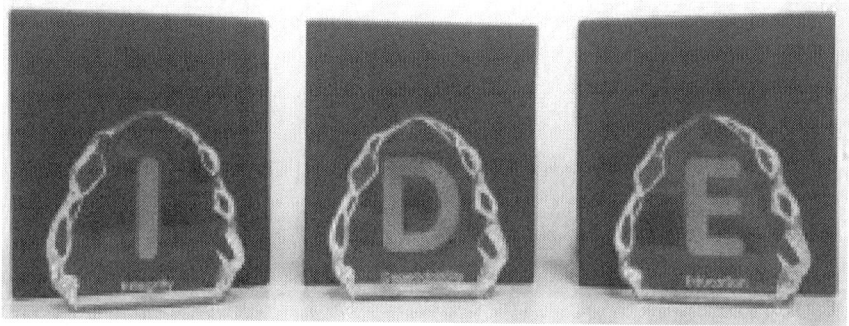

2. Shout Outs

In the daily team meeting, ask everyone to call out colleagues who are living the Core Values of the company.

> *"I would like to say thank you to Mary who ran a session after work to help us all understand the new billing system. Mary demonstrated our Education Core Value".*

Foundation Plan - Growth Plan

The Why?

Business growth typically only happens when you are intentional. By this, I mean that you have a plan documenting where you are heading and you are investing sufficient time and financial resources to making it happen.

If you consider that everyone is your potential customer your messages will always be vanilla, bland and instantly ignorable. By having a focus on an avatar customer type, you can start to hone your efforts which will improve their effectiveness.

The growth plan consists of working out who you serve, where you will obtain your lists of prospects, working out why you are unique, reassuring the prospects you are genuine, working out who you will be talking to and then having a plan as to how you can get your messages in front of these prospects.

Finally, the growth plan will be your chance to document the process of bringing a prospect on as a customer. This document can be shared with prospects. You may even find this openness could become one of your unique attributes.

This part of the plan is very much about them and not about you. As you write it, think about what would enhance the chance of winning the business and retaining the customer for the long term.

This process will not create a marketing plan on its own but will at least give you some top line detail to aim your marketing plan towards.

You can in time have more than one avatar, but the general advice on this is to ensure you have a working process serving one avatar well before you repeat this process to address another business sector.

Method

Work through each of these sections in order, detailing your output into the Foundation Plan document.

Avatar - Sector - Think about who you serve well today, resulting in happy customers and those that your staff understand well and like to work with. Work out which customers deliver you the best profitability after you have deducted all cost of goods and the labour costs to manage them. You are looking for a sector that has growth capacity, so avoid the temptation to focus on your existing 'unicorn' customers. When you answer this, think of a high-level business grouping.

Examples:

- *Manufacturing.*
- *Professional Services.*
- *Financial.*
- *Retail.*
- *Tourism.*
- *Media.*
- *Public Sector Organisations.*
- *Charities.*

Avatar - Size – What's the smallest company you can serve and still deliver both profitably and against your purpose? Would a one-man-band be able to take your business advice and buy into your solutions? What's the largest company you can credibly serve before the prospect sees you as too small to deliver? You will be at risk if you get this wrong, so give this one some thought. I find the employee count an easy one to discuss with prospects compared to revenue.

Examples

- *New business start-ups.*
- *Fewer than 20 employees.*
- *Between 20 and 100 employees.*
- *Between £2M and £10M revenue.*
- *Any FTSE listed blue-chip companies.*

Avatar - Geography – In this 'remote world' you can kid yourself that everywhere is serviceable by your business, but how wide can you spread your marketing message and still be heard. Think very carefully as to whether your business should be a shark in a paddling pool or a minnow in the ocean. What is the impact to your business of trying to service a wider geographical area than needed to achieve your growth goals?

Examples

- *Within 30 miles of our office.*
- *Within a 60-minute drive of our office.*
- *Within our county.*
- *Within our postcode area.*
- *Within our defined map.*

List Building – So now you have an avatar, you need to create a list of prospect companies. How many companies matching your avatar (sector, size and geography) are there? How can you compile a list of the companies that match your avatar? When you start to drive marketing activity, a shorter list of the right companies that match your avatar will deliver greater and more focus on results than a massive list being approached in a scattergun way.

Examples

- *Credit checking agencies.*
- *List brokers.*
- *Published top companies to work for lists.*
- *Help from your accountant.*
- *Local knowledge.*
- *Local business news.*
- *Internet research.*

Unique – So why would your avatar consider you to be the de facto choice when it comes to selecting new providers. Try to list up to three things that are not common to other suppliers like you as they service this avatar. Ideally, you are aiming for unique differences and avoid listing things like "we are better" or "we deliver quality" as those are very subjective and can't be conveyed in marketing messages. This will be a difficult session to complete, but worth the effort as if what makes you unique is in demand by your prospects, you have an easy route to gain their attention within your marketing efforts. What makes your customer feel safe, special and valued?

Examples

- *Investment in team skills development.*
- *Industry sector dedicated therefore greater knowledge.*
- *Account management process.*
- *Cheapest provider.*
- *Fastest service.*
- *24/7 Provision.*
- *Client onboarding process.*
- *Employee-owned.*
- *Locally sourced or proven provenance products.*

Guarantee – How can you reassure your prospects that what you say you can deliver confidently. You may call this a pledge or promise. This is a step towards setting the expectations of your customer.

Examples

- *The first response to service requests within 15 minutes.*
- *Proposals supplied within 48 hours.*
- *Never beaten on price.*

Personas – Who within these companies are you going to need to connect with to do business with them? Is it the managing director or the service users within the organisation? You need to understand who makes the ultimate buying decision but also who are the influencers of those decisions. The chances are there are a few different groups of people you need to define here. Give them a friendly name and write down who you think they are and what they care about. Once you have these defined, you will be able to create your marketing messages to address each of these personas with a language and message that will resonate with what they care about.

Examples
- *Simon – Business Owner – Cares about profit, reputation and customer satisfaction.*
- *Freda – Finance Director – Cares about managing costs and planned budgets.*
- *Dave – Operations Manager – Cares about quality and service.*

Communication Strategy – Now you have a good idea of who you want to speak with, you need a plan as to how to best get in front of those people on a per persona basis. You need to think about how you can be where those people will be.

Examples
- *Seminars in conjunction with their professional body.*
- *Direct connection on LinkedIn or other social media.*
- *Attend exhibitions for their sector.*
- *Create knowledge events for their sector.*

Foundation Plan - Medium Term Plan

The Why?

This section of the foundation plan model is designed to ensure that every year counts towards your goal. Without a plan, it is easy for each year to look pretty much the same.

You will still achieve something, but it may not be the thing you needed to achieve. More importantly, your team don't know what's in your head so this is a way to communicate your expectations.

In discussion, I sometimes call the medium-term plan the 'Value creation strategy' but realise for business owners desperate for more sales they make the jump to this being about increasing short term profit or even worse, the vanity mistake of just chasing an increase in revenue.

The value and success of your business long term are about so much more than just revenue or profit, but it is built on your people, process and accreditations.

There are two parts to this plan and you will need to trust me that there is value in following the process exactly.

- **Step One** – Define where you are heading.
- **Step Two** – Document the gap between where you are today and where you want to be.

Method

Populate the Foundation Plan template with a summary of the details you create during this process.

Step One

The first step is to paint a picture of the future with words. Start by creating a date in the future. It's important that this plan is short enough to create a positive pressure on you and your team and remain within view, this side of the cognitive horizon, but also long enough to allow you to be strategic in your thinking and able to achieve some impressive projects.

Typically, this should be somewhere between three and five years. You should review this plan annually and where required rewrite this plan to keep it relevant.

Example
- *Future Date – End of 2023*

Picture yourself at that date in the future and enjoy what it's like as you review what you have achieved. Write that down in the current tense. 'We consistently score 97% customer satisfaction' or 'We serve 30% of the available market'. Try and think about all areas of the business as you get creative.

Thinking about where you want to be will allow you to visualise how it feels to achieve, but also helps you understand what you need to do to get there.

Example
- *The data in our line of business application is always accurate.*
- *We hold current competencies in our top three vendors programmes.*
- *Our staff enjoy a fair and transparent pay and reward structure.*
- *We look after 30 customers within a one-hour drive of our office.*
- *We receive 4x organic leads each month from our marketing investment.*
- *The standard operating procedure for onboarding is used every time.*

And finally, let's get the finance numbers into this plan.

EXAMPLE
- *Turnover – £2M revenue at 15% net profit.*

Step Two

The goals are best split into categories, for which I would suggest infrastructure, accreditations, process, people & growth. You may have some other headings to create even more clarity.

Now you have a view of the future defined, you need to pull out the SMART goals. It helps to compartmentalise these into categories as you document them.

If any of your goals will take more than about 3-months to complete, I recommend you break them down into smaller goals. These are sometimes called milestone goals and in which case, each milestone will also be **SMART**.

For the want of clarity, the definition in this book for that acronym is:

- **Specific** – No confusion. Anyone can read and understand it too.
- **Measurable** – You will know when you have achieved. Ideally a number.
- **Achievable** – You have the time and financial resource to succeed.
- **Relevant** – Is this going to help you deliver your business mission?
- **Timebound** – When will this goal be started and when will it be complete?

The next step is to document the gap between where you are today and your view of the future by way of structured goals. At this point, you don't need to determine which of your team resources will own these goals. That will come later in your leadership and team appraisal process, where each team member will have goals that are aligned to this medium-term plan.

You will notice that **'The data in our line of business application is always accurate.'** from my example on the previous page creates more than one goal in the example list. As you consider each of your future statements there will be some people related goals around training and development.

Example:

Infrastructure
- *Replace line of business application by the end of 2021.*

Accreditations
- *Create three teams of two colleagues and provide them scheduled time to gain competency in our top three vendor programmes by Jun 21.*

Process Goals
- *Review and update customer onboarding process by Apr 21*

People Goals
- *Define pay and reward structure based on metrics by Mar 21.*
- *Train onboarding staff on the updated process during May 21.*
- *Train all account managers to deliver the new process by May 21.*
- *Structured training in our line of business application by Aug 21.*
- *Staff onboarding to include the line of business training by Sep 21.*

Growth Goals
- *Create an annual plan of monthly electronic, physical and in-person content aimed at the personas within the avatar customers by Feb 21.*
- *Deliver this marketing plan consistently throughout the year.*
- *Turnover growth at 10% to get from £1.5M to £2M by end of 2023*
- *Sign up one new customer based on the avatar each quarter.*
- *Improve net profit from 10% to 15% by end of 2023 by:*
    - *Review pricing to improve unit profitability by Feb 21.*
    - *Review business costs by Mar 21.*
    - *Account management process for cross-selling by May 21.*

Foundation Plan - Long Term Plan

The Why?

This is the toughest one to define but arguably the most important to invest some thinking time, as this is your 'exit plan'. What we need to talk about here is your legacy. What you leave behind. Let me assure you, at some point, you will exit your business even if they carry you out in a box.

This section is about what happens to the business after you no longer can or want to own it.

Before you proceed, let's discuss the impact of not talking about business succession.

- Your team will make up their minds as to what is going to happen and it's likely to at best be a distraction from your goals and at worst something that will sabotage your plans. It's amazing what people dream up and assume to fill the void of silence.

- The end will come quicker than you expect. Some business exits will take more preparation than others, so your chances of success improve the sooner you give this some thought. If you don't have the structure or leadership skills in place you limit your exit options.

So, with an understanding of the need for a succession plan, the next page works through the timeline, financials, skills and finally a discussion on types of exit you could consider.

Method

How much of this you put into your one-page foundation plan will be determined by how open you want to be with your employees, but you must work through all these steps to understand the enormity of the responsibility you have at this time.

Timeline – When are you planning to exit your business? For me, I always planned to exit on my 50th birthday and I did. That was a specific goal from when I left my last employer on the day of my 21st birthday. For you, this could be 5 or even 25 years away but put something down.

Example
> 1. *June 2025 on my 50th birthday – 5 years.*

Financials – Do you want to achieve financial independence when you leave the business? If so, how much money do you need from your exit to provide that? How much is your business worth today? There are effectively four parts to this element, which you will work through in order.

1. **Personal Wealth Required** – So keeping with the example of a 50-year-old it's probably prudent to expect to live to at least 80 years old. As such, you have 30 years' worth of life to pay for. The spend is probably not a straight line, but one that looks more like this where the early years still have posh holidays, flash cars and maybe a wedding or two to fund. The middle years are where things get a little quieter with there being a limit to what you will spend on OAP coach trips. The final peak will be when your medical care costs increase. You will also want to include the value of your final home (which may or may not be the one you live in today).

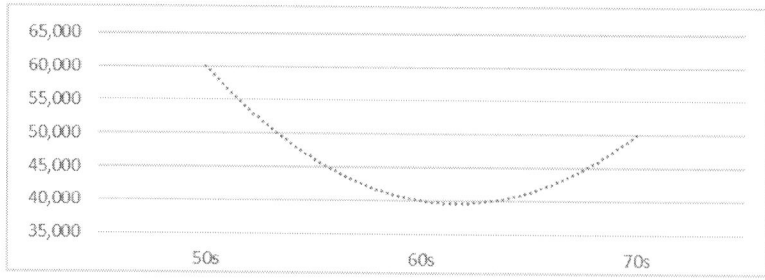

Example
> *10 years @ £60K, 10 years @ 40K, 10 years @ 50K plus a £500K bungalow by the sea, so £2M total.*

2. **Current Personal Wealth** – So now you know how much wealth you need to accumulate, you need to work through how far along you are, or rather how much you will have accumulated by your planned exit date. At this point exclude the value of your business, but include your pension, savings and equity in your current home.

Example

Pension - £300K, Savings – £100K, House Equity - £400K. This equals a total worth £800K and therefore a personal wealth shortfall of £1.2M.

3. **Business Current Valuation** – It is often said that valuing a business is subjective and mostly driven by market forces. You will also hear that a business is worth 'what someone is willing to pay for it'. That is partially right but shouldn't stop you from having a way to value the business every year so you can see if you are heading in the right direction. Your business sector will have its multipliers to calculate the value and your accountant can probably help you here. The value of your business consists of the future trade (usually an average of a multiplier of your annual profit and a percentage of your revenue) plus the value of your balance sheet retained profits from previous years performance. When selling adjustment will also be made for client contracts, vertical markets and owner add-backs or deductions. Let's presume you pay yourself as Managing Director what it would cost to hire a Managing Director and you can ignore these adjustments at this point, as it will confuse the purpose of this valuation. For the example here, I will use the IT sector which for businesses turning over less than £3 million in revenue typically values at about a 5x multiplier of EBITDA averaged with 60% of the revenue.

Example

Revenue £1.5M and an EBITDA of £150K with a balance sheet value of £50K
Value Method 1 - Multiplier Model - £150K x 5 = £750K value
Value Method 2 - 60% of revenue = £900K value
Average of £750K and £900K = £825K trade valuation.
Then add the balance sheet of £50K = £875K

4. **Identify the Gap** – If the plan is that your business is going to provide financial independence, you need to work out the gap between what the business is worth today and what you need it to be worth by the time you reach the date you proposed at the start of this exercise. If you have business partners you will need to adjust for how much of the sale proceeds will be coming your way too. You will also need to factor in taxation as the figures you created earlier for your personal need are after income tax.

Example

Continuing with the same example and in this case, assuming you would be able to gain entrepreneurs capital gain relief bringing the tax rate down to 10% on your exit.

You need £1.2M on exit. Therefore, your business needs to be worth about £1.35M before 10% tax for you to walk away with £1.2M

Today the business is worth £875K so you need to add a further £475K within 5 years. Assuming a straight line, if you can increase the value of the business by just £95K per year, every year for 5 years you will reach your target business valuation. Therefore, you will need to increase your EBITDA by about £20K year on year for the five years you have left.

Skills - Can your business run without you today? Often business owners tell me about how great their leadership team are, but often they are only great at holding the line rather than great at seeing how the business needs to continue to develop. Consider the following list of tasks that require decision making.

- Ideation and investment in the next big thing
- Selection of company software
- Handling customer complaints
- Signing up new customers
- Agreeing to discounts with customers
- Firing non-compliant customers
- Hiring new staff for growth
- Firing non-performing staff
- Authorising marketing costs
- Authorising capital investment for assets
- Changes to bank accounting provider
- Managing supplier relationships
- Implementing a price increase across existing customers
- Setting the company budget

Which of these can your leadership team undertake without needing to seek any additional authorisation from you to complete? List the names of who in your team has been empowered to make each of these types of decision, of course assuming they are following the process required to make that decision.

Once you have completed this exercise any task that doesn't have at least two names (not including the owners) will need a plan to create or refine, a standard operating procedure and then empower the leadership team to be able to step up.

Most decision-making skills can be learned through culture and process, but if these decisions are coming back to you as the business owner there is almost certainly more work for you to do as you approach any kind of business exit.

One final comment about this is that although this is a section about exiting your business, having more than one person in your business able to handle everything in your absence is also just great continuity planning.

Exit – There are many ways to exit a business. The options available to you will be determined partially by your answers to the questions about financials and skills in the previous exercises.

Here is a simple summary of seven exits for you to consider.

1. **Trade Sale** – This is the most common type of business exit and includes the usual buyer-seller dance whilst you negotiate both the price and how much of the payment is on sale day and how much is part of an 'earn out' effectively funded by the future trade of the business. It is not uncommon for the exiting owners to be expected to work for a period after the sale. The earn-out often has clauses to protect the buyer should the business not deliver as well as it had been inferred during the sale process.

2. **Management Buy-Out** – This is less discussed but is where your senior staff raise capital to buy the owners out. Less haggling of course but is dependent on the staff having the financial standing to raise the money and their success dependant on how structured the management team are. Four people buying you out who all want to be Managing Director will create new tensions that the team have not needed to deal with.

3. **Employee Ownership** – This is similar to the management buy-out option but is where you effectively pass the business over to all the staff in return for future profits. This type of exit is not right for you if you need a large amount of cash in one go or if you are risk-averse. It is however the least 'bumpy' for everyone and currently the most tax-efficient.

4. **Family Succession** – If you have children that have been groomed to take over the business, my advice would be to ensure they have their feet under the boardroom table long enough to gain the full respect of the team. What you negotiate as a 'sale' value will probably not be based on any of the methods I have discussed in this section.

5. **Absent Owner** – This is a kind of exit strategy, but basically if you have a business that sort of runs itself, you can just not go to work leaving the team to do their own thing. Your lunch breaks get longer and you get to take more holidays. If the company leadership can make great decisions without you, this could run forever but the challenge comes when things change that the team are not already prepared to deal with or they start to feel you are vacuuming up too much of 'their' hard-earned profits. If that happens, will you have the appetite to come back in and fix things or will that be stressful?

6. **Private Equity or Venture Capital** – For some sectors, there are options to sell your business to organisations who are looking to 'buy and build' where your customer base will be added to one larger company they are creating. This type of exit requires the least preparation work for you, but this type of acquisition also typically creates quite a few employee casualties, so you may need to check your morals at the front door!

7. **Initial Public Offering (IPO)** – If your business is much bigger 'floating' on the public stock exchanges may be an option. Typically for IPOs to work you need to have a revenue of upwards of £50M and be able to demonstrate a large growth potential for your business.

Once you have an idea of the type of exit you plan, work with your business coach to document the pros and cons. Once you are sure you have picked the right option and assuming you are ready to share your plans, it may be best to get your leadership team involved in the process of preparing for your exit and mitigating any risks that are involved in your plan.

Foundation Plan – Wider Perspective

The Why?

This is the final but essential part of the Foundation Plan. It is made up of two components.

1. **Working On** - How much do you work on, rather than in your business?
2. **Hanging Out** - Who do you spend time with that influences your thinking?

Typically, when businesses are starting up, the owner is committed to working all the hours just to stand still. Just to make ends meet. All too often, that way of working becomes a habit. Even when the business has reached some modicum of success, the owner still chooses to spend most of their time working within the business.

Without an understanding and a plan for the two questions at the start of this chapter, you will lack a wider perspective. Symptoms of this include:

- **Stalled Growth** – The level of thinking that got the business going, won't sustain growth.
- **Reducing Profit** – With a lack of growth and rising costs, profit disappears.
- **Fire Fighting** – Only things at crisis point get any attention.
- **Quality Control** – Little by little, processes fail and the quality of output deteriorates.

This chapter will cover off the following seven important topics that will help you create a process to gain a wider perspective:

1. **Prioritisation**
2. **Improvement**
3. **Reflection**
4. **Environment**
5. **Accountability**
6. **Peer Groups**
7. **Stories**

Method

Each of these topics will require you to do some work as you follow the steps to better understand how you spend your time today and how you could spend your time in future. This will ensure you are always able to gain and understand a wider perspective.

1. Prioritisation

Not all tasks are the same. You need to understand the difference between urgent and important. Learn how to schedule and stop thinking short term. No more firefighting. Improve your delegation skills.

I know that this will make me appear unsympathetic, but when people say to me *'I have no time to do that'*, I hear, *'I am very poor at managing my time and don't know how to prioritise. Please help me!'*. The point here is that we all have the same 168 hours each week. It's how we choose to spend them. It's my choice to invest 3-hours each day at the desk in my study working on my writing.

If nobody has shown you an alternative way, the good news is that it's not your fault that right now you are making excuses rather than making a difference.

Exercise Step One – What do you do?

Write a high-level headline list of everything you do at work for the next week that takes you more than 10 minutes. You don't need to be any more granular right now for the first round of this exercise and hopefully, you will be able to capture at least 70% of your working day. Your list may look something like this, albeit hopefully quite a bit longer:

Example
- *Opened the post.*
- *Reviewed three quotations before sales can send them to clients.*
- *Visited an unhappy client to reassure them things are improving.*
- *Sifted through the new CVs received for a current vacancy.*
- *Rearranged paper clips in the stationery cupboard.*
- *Planning work for the staff outing to celebrate the 10th anniversary.*
- *Attended staff disciplinary.*

Exercise Step Two – Should you be doing it?

The next step is to understand that not all tasks are the same and to help with that I would like to introduce you to the Eisenhower Matrix.

As you may gather from the unusual name, this tool is credited to Dwight D Eisenhower, the 34th president of the United States. A busy man who realised that his time needed to be invested into making only the decisions that could not be made by others.

	Urgent	Not Urgent
Important	**1. Do First** First focus on important tasks to be done the same day.	**2. Schedule** Important, but not-so-urgent tasks should be scheduled.
Not Important	**3. Delegate** What's urgent, but less important, delegate to others.	**4. Don't Do** What's neither urgent nor important, don't do at all.

Every task you completed last week can be easily categorised into one of these four distinct quadrants.

When I say 'Important' I don't mean important that it happens, but important that you do it yourself. When you get your time management sorted, you will only undertake tasks that are either in quadrant 1 or 2.

Quadrant 1 – For people with poor time management, this is the busiest box. Typically, this will be filled with other peoples 'can you just do this' type of jobs. Of course, there are genuine things that need to be in this box where your life or career depends on your input.

Quadrant 2 – This is the most practical box and where anything you can schedule goes. Removing the urgent removes stress. For example, writing a book like this one only happens because I schedule the time in an appropriate environment to be conducive to writing. This box is the most efficient and effective quadrant. This is where you will make a difference within your business.

Quadrant 3 – This is where it gets tough. There are things you do today that you feel that only you can undertake. You may be right, but that needs to change. You need to start looking at what you can delegate safely to enable you to work on the things that are important so that you can do them instead. This will of course involve an element of training, but this effort on your part will repay you handsomely as you can reclaim time that you can use more efficiently for scheduled quadrant 2 tasks.

Quadrant 4 – Well, those YouTube clips of cats aren't going to watch themselves, now are they? Seriously as you look at the tasks that you undertook you will find that sometimes you were your own worst enemy. Losing an afternoon that started with great intentions of checking your Google reviews and ended with you touching base with your old school chums on Facebook until home time. This is not going to help you reach your success goals, so you need to wean yourself off. An end of day reward maybe would be better than starting straight after lunch!

As you progress with this exercise, the next stage is to look deeper into the tasks you undertook last week and determine which quadrant they should be categorised as. I have added a notes column to my example so you can see my thinking as I determined their quadrant. You can do the same with your list:

Task Details	Notes	Quadrant
Opened the post.	Easily delegated.	3. Urgent, Not Important
Reviewed three quotations before sales can send them to clients.	With authority and training, the Sales Manager can be given some autonomy to complete this.	3. Urgent, Not Important
Visited an unhappy client to reassure them things are improving.	If only you can placate this customer, it may be that you need to drop everything and attend.	1. Urgent, Important
Sifted through the new CVs received for a current vacancy.	The first pass of the CVs could be delegated to the line manager.	3. Urgent, Not Important
Rearranged paper clips in the stationery cupboard.	Does it matter if this never happens? You were doing it to feel useful. Don't do it again!	4. Not Urgent, Not Important
Planning work for the staff outing to celebrate the 10th anniversary.	You enjoy giving to your team and love to plan a party. You want to do this and the team will appreciate your efforts.	2. Not Urgent, Important
Attended staff disciplinary.	You have a responsibility to attend this meeting, but it will be scheduled.	2. Not Urgent, Important

From now, as new activities appear in your task list, use what you have learned today together with this decision-making flowchart to determine which quadrant the task fits into and do it, schedule it, delegate it or just don't do it!

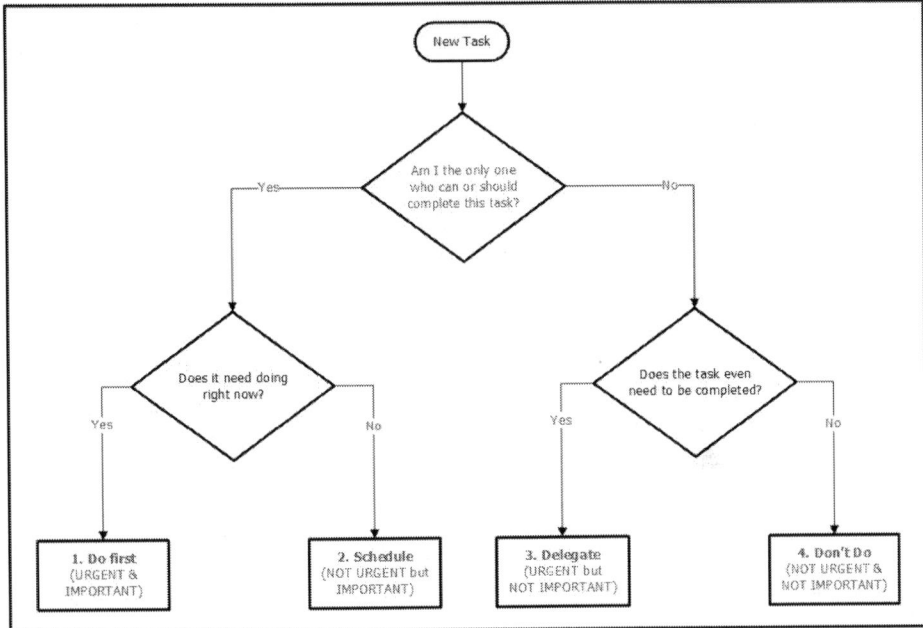

Exercise Step Three – Not all time is of the same value

As I mentioned, quadrant 2 time is the most efficient and effective. This next step is just a little more advanced but worth giving some consideration to at this point, now you have mastered categorising your tasks.

Not all scheduled time is equal. Let's look at next weeks proposed schedule.

- **Monday** – Working from home and covering childcare issues.
- **Tuesday** – Working from the office all day.
- **Wednesday** – Working from home alone all day.
- **Thursday** – Visiting clients around the county.
- **Friday** – Playing golf.

On the face of this, Monday, Tuesday and Wednesday all look like great times to schedule quadrant 2 tasks and of course, Thursday and Friday are not. This is where some people struggle with time management as the stage that they miss is to rate the quality of their available time. As I look at next week, I can see that Monday is likely to have some interruptions from the children and Tuesday interruptions from the staff. The only amazing day to make strides in achievement will be Wednesday. Home alone.

I use a traffic light system to help me easily see the value of the time I am using to schedule my tasks. If it's Red, I can't schedule anything. If it's Amber, I can schedule only the type of tasks that I know won't matter if they are interrupted. My precious Green time is where I may switch off the world and write without fear of interruption.

With this knowledge, I schedule my tasks based on their need for quality time. I have a task to work alongside my panel of proofreaders. That's very much about correspondence. I have found that I can dip in and out of that task so I can complete it well in my Amber time.

Which of your scheduled tasks do you need quality time away from interruptions and which can you do around your employees or children?

Mastering the prioritisation of your time is a foundation plan element because without this, you just won't be able to allocate the time you need to complete the other 28 sections in this book.

2. Improvement

This book is taking you on a journey to consider the 34 most important sets of processes any successful business needs. However, it's critical to understand that business success is an iterative process. By which I mean, you can always do better. The reason for the scoring rubric at the start of this book is to help you understand where in your business you should be focussing your attention next.

Once you have your processes in place, you need to review them regularly to ensure they are still fit for purpose and delivering as expected. If they are not, you need to take steps to modify your processes and deploy and train your team as required to ensure the changes are effective.

To ensure you have reviewed each process at least annually, consider scheduling time to review just three processes each month. Create a list of the processes you have in a table and add when you first created the document and the date you plan to review it. Schedule the time now even if it's not happening for another 12 months.

Today you may be the owner of all your processes, but over time you will start to delegate authority for owning these processes to your leadership team. Again, complete that column.

Lastly, these processes don't exist in a vacuum. As you create and review processes, pull together the team. Not all processes will require the same team members, but ensure you have sufficient stakeholders across all levels of the business to ensure what you create resonates well with the team. This improves your chances of success as you implement any changes to processes.

Process	Issued	Review	Owner	Team
Purpose, Vision & Mission				
Core Values				
Growth Plan				
Medium Term Plan				
Long Term Plan				
Wider Perspective				

3. Reflection

Being responsible for a business and a group of employees is an enormous burden and hopefully an honour. You have hungry mouths to feed and people who look to you for guidance. It's your task to ensure there is a clear direction being followed that will result in there being work and wages for many years ahead.

The question here is, are you doing enough to be the best version of yourself. Your employees deserve at least that from you and your business success depends on it. Taking time out to think always seems indulgent. Such as any time that could be better invested in a more active and 'doing' role. Nothing could be more incorrect.

The great news here is that you are reading my book. Don't stop at the end of this book. There is a world of great business books out there that will energise and inspire you. My advice to you is to cascade the learning to your leadership and employees. Some books need a complete read to make sense, but sometimes books can be boiled down to just the valuable content for your environment into a few slides to teach at the next team meeting.

Moving on from learning from books, it is also your role to set the company vision. Is it defined well enough? Are the goals you are progressing today going to deliver against your vision? What do you stand for and what do you stand against? Can you better define your niche?

Look at your schedule for the last quarter and document how much time you spent either on your own or with your leadership team reflecting on what you have achieved and what you need to achieve in the future.

In addition to my own time to think, within my previous technology business, we had one day aside every quarter reserved for strategy. In fact, as the Chairman these are the only meetings I still regularly attend. All operational or tactical topics are off-limits. The only things allowed on the agenda are bigger picture views of the next steps for the company.

This meeting is attended by the leadership team plus two people from the employee council to ensure their voice is heard at this strategic direction level. In addition, if there is a topic that will impact an area of the business additional colleagues are brought into the meeting as required.

The agenda for the meeting is pre-set and communicated ahead of the meeting and there is often some pre-work to be completed. Often thinking related. It ensures that when we meet the ideas can flow freely. The strategic meetings are some of the best time that is invested in the future success of the business. In 2020 we learned that these meetings work well virtually too.

Your task here is to schedule time for your thinking. And then schedule time for working on your business from a strategic view together with the stakeholders of your business.

4. Environment

This seems like an odd topic and I won't take up too much of your time here but where is the best place to think? When it comes to your thinking time, is that when you are walking the dog across the field or sitting in a darkened room. You need to know what environment is conducive to your ability to focus.

As to your company strategy meetings, some people can't switch into a strategic mode if they are at the same desk where they do their operational day-to-day function. Offsite meetings can have great value especially as you introduce the discipline of strategic meetings. Remember, this is not about you but about getting the best from the team's time investment.

5. Accountability

As I started on my journey of writing this, I talked to my long-time business friends about my book proposal. They asked me questions like "Is there a market for the book", "How much time will it take?", "When will it be complete?" and fortunately also "How can I help?" and "When can I get a copy?".

These questions were foundational for me to commit the time and energy required to turn the thoughts that were in my head into the book that is now in your hand. I am grateful to every one of my critical friends who were willing to ask the awkward questions, whilst offering me support.

Who makes you feel awkward?

When I restarted my career as a mentor, I used the tagline 'Critical Friend'. There is something about caring for the success of others so much, you are willing to be critical with your advice. And of course, in a mentoring role, the mentee must know that you are offering your critical advice with good intentions.

If today you don't have a coach or mentor in your support team consider getting one. Evaluate your progress each quarter and understand that you may need to change who you contract for this support to keep things fresh and ensure activity is being driven by their engagement.

Without a formal coach or mentor, you can still be selective about which friends you trust to give you advice. It's easy to surround yourself with people who are like you and who like you. These are not always the people who will be candid with their analysis of your proposals or your progress. Where you don't need to explain this to a professional, if you choose to turn an existing friend or business contact into your informal mentor, it's your job to set the ground rules about how honest you need them to be.

Who is going to hold you accountable?

6. Peer Groups

Firstly, when I say peer groups, I do not mean networking groups. Many networking groups meet over breakfast, lunch or dinner with the primary objective of passing business enquiries. Depending on your business sector these can form a great marketing pillar but do not feature in this section of the book.

The type of peer group I am talking about is a meeting of equals. A group of like-minded business leaders who regularly take time out of their businesses to meet with you and work on your business. Essentially, those who are willing to put the needs of others ahead of their own. Are you that kind of person too?

Again, there are many peer groups out there. Here are a few considerations for when you are looking to join one:

- **Sector Aligned** – Some peer groups are cross-sector and others aligned to your industry. Sector-based ones mean you don't need to explain what you do in your business so your peers can help you. Although cross-sector alternatives can bring some wider perspectives than the blinkered view of your sector.

- **Benchmarking** – Some sector-based peer groups create benchmarking systems allowing you to compare your company finance or operational performance to others in your sector. This helps you understand if your business is performing as well as it could with empirical data rather than opinion.

- **Competition** – For most sectors, there is plenty of work that is won by the best providers. Having one of your competitors in a peer group with you is typically not a terrible thing as the rules of the peer group will normally forbid them from approaching your customers. Of course, not all business people are ready to have that kind of open dialogue and are still fearful of their competitors.

- **Frequency** – How often the group meets will drive activity. There is always a flurry of activity in the run-up to a meeting so monthly meetings create monthly activity. If the group meets infrequently, don't expect much activity to come from your group.

- **Scale** – If your business is growing and the rest of your peer's businesses are not, you may need to change your group to continue your growth. It's OK that the people in the group are your friends, but they are no longer helping you as they are no longer your peers. Your equals. Understand when it's time to find a peer group that is made up of the right size businesses with the same shared growth goals.

- **Cost** – Of course, how much you need to pay will always be a factor. Like when reviewing your choice of mentor keep a close watch on how much progress you are making by being a member of a peer group. If you can't justify the costs, find a better way to invest your money.

7. Stories

The last section of gaining a wider perspective is about stories. Life is made up of stories and anyone who knows me, knows I love to tell a story. Stories bring ideas alive if you can tell them with passion.

When you watch comedians, so many of their stories are based on real-life observations. That's what makes them interesting to listen to and relatable. They draw you in. The conclusion for a comedian is typically an amusing punchline. I remember going to a Tim Vine gig in Edinburgh one wet and windy evening where he drifted across everyone seated in the front row asking what people did for a living. He was able to tell a story with a joke at the end for everyone he spoke with about their profession.

Business stories are quite similar. They need to be interesting, drawing you in and they of course need a conclusion. A purpose as to why you started out telling them the story.

The wider perspective section of this book is also about improving your story listening. You are exposing yourself to more stories and more storytellers. To take advantage of this, I challenge you to take notes.

Don't assume your memory will be good enough. Then think about how you can relate what you have learned to retell it as your story to your team or customers like I have just told you about my time with Tim Vine. You have permission to adapt your story to your audience or embellish and add whatever drama you need to ensure it is engaging.

Company-Wide – Organisational Chart

The Why?

An Organisational Chart, or Organogram, is a diagram to show relationships and authority for reporting as a structure within your business.

When I hear the phrase **"we have a flat structure"**, typically I will subsequently learn that there is an accidental structure in place, that is nothing like flat. Often when a company has grown to more than 10 staff and they all still report directly to the owner it's a sign of other challenges such as a fear of losing control.

So why do business owners have an unwillingness to get this down on paper?

- A desire to avoid awkward conversations about the mismatch between the business owners view of the organisation and what the employees have assumed.
- A mistaken belief that no structure provides a dynamic ability to change as needed allowing you to repurpose your employees on a whim.
- The relationships between the employees are too complicated to map into a diagram because some employees have lots of areas of responsibility.

You will be better off with a documented organisation chart because:

- It will be easier for new employees to settle in, understanding who they report to and who has responsibility for their induction and training?
- It is easier to create meaningful standard operating procedures when they are tied to the functions of a job role.
- Creating a disaster recovery plan for your employees is easier if you know what each of your employees does.

The six-step process within this book to create a working functional organisation chart.

1. Define a role-based structure.
2. Define the functions under each role.
3. Document standard operating procedures.
4. Map your employees.
5. Assign understudies for all roles.
6. Share the completed diagram with your whole team.

Method

I need you to stop thinking top-down and start thinking bottom-up.

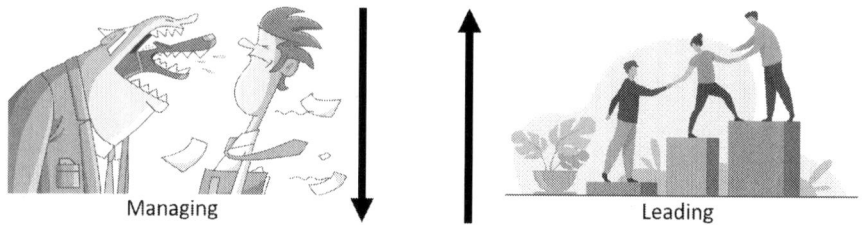

Managing   Leading

By this, I mean stop thinking of an organisational chart as a way for a manager to know who they can bark at to do a task. Instead, think about who an employee can look up to for guidance and who in that structure is there to help them achieve and be the best version of themselves.

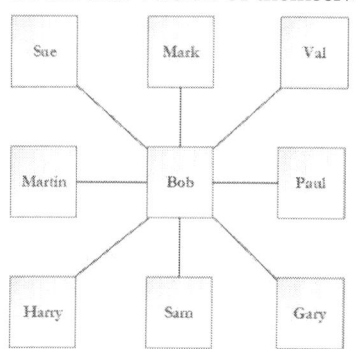

For most, the first organisational chart that the staff would draw would probably look like these spokes around a wheel with Bob, the managing director securely in the middle.

Sadly, this is not how Bob wishes the organisation works. He somehow believes that Sam, Mark and Val have some responsibility.

Maybe this has not been communicated clearly to either those three leaders or the five direct reports that have been entrusted to them.

Typically, if today Sam, Mark and Val are not stepping up to their responsibility to lead and develop their direct reports it will be the result of one or more of these four things.

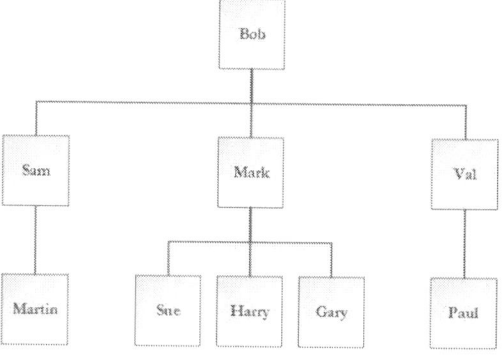

1. They don't know WHO they have responsibility for.
2. They don't know WHY the company's success depends on this happening.
3. They don't know HOW to lead their team.
4. Or, Bob has historically undermined any effort they have made so they have given up.

The answers to bringing clarity for No 1 will be answered in this chapter and No 2 & 3 will be resolved over time with leadership training and support from Bob.

No 4 is the biggest challenge and is down to Bob changing what has now probably become deeply engrained awful habits. Once he realises that he is the weak link to growing his business, he will gain a desire to make the change. It starts with learning to trust his trained and motivated leaders to take control of their teams.

It is also not unusual with this type of organisational chart to end up with 'dotted lines' joining where perhaps Sue also works for Sam and Val in some function. Let's call what she does a generic term like 'Admin'. This shared resource causes confusion and frustration.

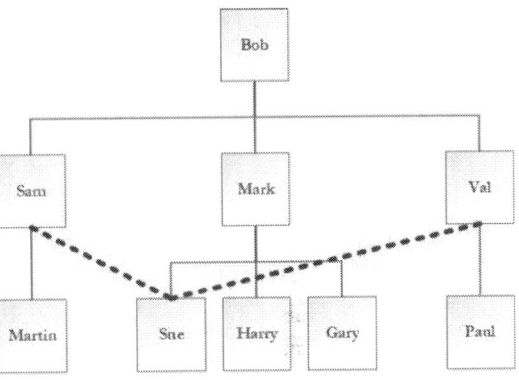

How should Sue prioritise her day? Who should she turn to for advice, Mark, Sam or Val?

Once Bob starts getting involved too, Sue doesn't stand a chance. Sue's job ends up with more stress than she deserves. Let's fix that challenge too.

Finally, this type of organisational chart doesn't scale well either. Let's look at Sue again. What happens if her Admin job becomes too big for one person?

Where does the new person attach to this chart? The temptation is to make the recruit Sue's understudy. After all, Sue achieves so well, working for Mark, Sam and Val.

The type of chart we are going to define today will eliminate all the above conflicts and provide us with a much clearer view of expected future growth.

Stage One – Define a role-based structure

The hard part here is to pretend you don't have any employees today. Let us start with a blank sheet of paper. All we know at the start is that we have a leader. The big cheese. This is the person who will ultimately be responsible for any failures and as such will be fully invested in making sure all their direct reports are successful.

As a former managing director, I was always tempted to have lots of direct reports. I think that was down to how the business started.

I only achieved success when I cut my leadership team down to just a few people. Departmental or functional areas of the business.

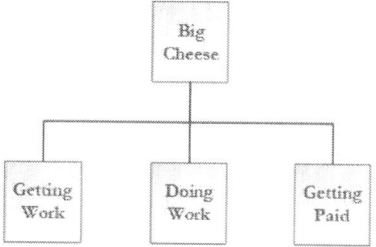

For me, this logically split into three business areas, namely getting work, doing work and making sure we were getting paid.

For additional clarity, this is how I defined the scope of these business areas.

- Big Cheese – Strategy & Vision.
- Getting Work – Marketing & Sales.
- Doing Work – Delivering your services.
- Getting Paid – Purchasing, Invoicing & Payroll

Each of these four roles has easy to measure success at a leadership level. This becomes even more important as you move towards salary structures that are based on business performance.

You may be able to justify other people on this top row of your leadership depending on your business sector, but what you are looking for in a role-based chart is accountability at the top-level leadership. Try not to separate interdependent roles (like Sales and Marketing or Purchasing and Invoicing) at this level.

The next step is to start adding the sub-roles. Think carefully about what you do in your business today and create your version of this chart. You will notice that within Bob's business, we have identified a need for an admin role in each of these functional areas of the business.

If you have plans to add new operational areas to your business, add the required boxes for those new roles too. Keep an eye on the future in this process as you should be planning for what your business will look like in 3-5 years, rather than just what you know today.

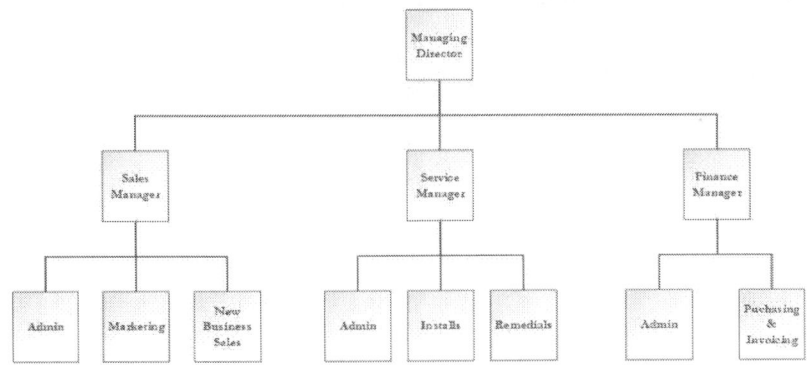

In our earlier example of Bob's company, we only have 9 people, but you can see that this drawing already has 12 identified roles. We will revisit this later in this process.

Stage Two – Define the functions under each role

Under each role, we now want to detail between four and six functions. These are the main things that the role will be responsible for within this structure and how you will measure success for the person in the role. Below is the functional chart for my old IT practice so you can see what a complete chart looks like at this point.

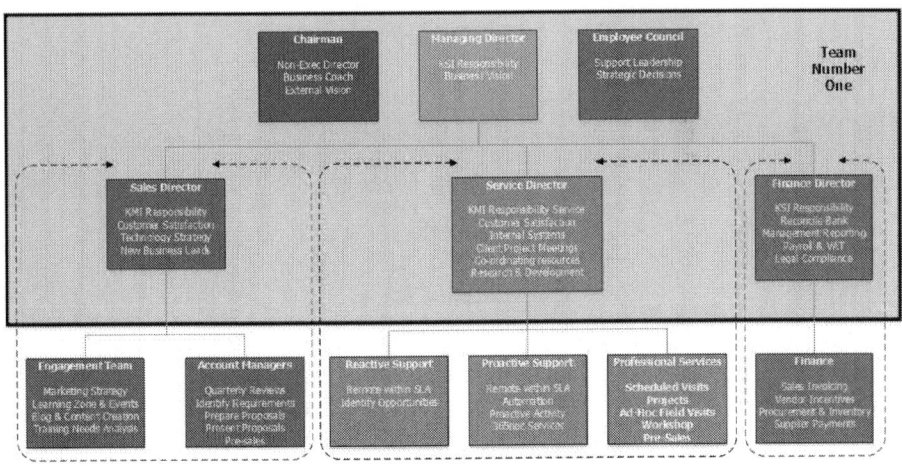

The top-level roles of the four directors plus the chairman and employee council make up team number one. It is this group that takes responsibility for the strategy, direction and overall performance of the business. This groups priority is collectively always the company vision.

Stage Three - Create standard operating procedures

Most people who document their operations into a set of standard operating procedures (or SOPs) do so to try and make their operation more consistent and repeatable. There are four other great reasons to take the time to document the processes which are:

- It makes training new starters who will deliver this function much simpler, quicker and more consistent.
- It provides a level of resilience should a member of staff go sick or leave. The stand-in employee can read the SOP documentation and become operational quickly.
- The action of documenting the SOPs makes you think about what you do today and why you do it. If your process is not optimal, it's a great time to adapt it.
- Finally, when things go wrong you can review the SOP and again adjust it or add in the extra stages that will make it more successful in future.

You will probably end up with SOPs for more than the functions than the ones on your organisational chart. The more the merrier, but only if they are kept up to date and used. Your review process for SOPs should include looking at all of them at least annually. I know that some people like to have lots of words to describe their process, but operationally I have found that a simple step-by-step flowchart is an easy and quick way to communicate a process at a high level.

For that reason, you will notice them cropping up quite often in this book. Again, borrowing heavily from my old business, on the next page is an example SOP for handling the monthly customer satisfaction survey prize purchase and award.

To accelerate the pace of going from having no SOPs to having one for everything, we decided to make this a job for our next new employee.

Having put the first document together as an example, we tasked the new employee to sit with their colleagues and document what they do into a flowchart.

Within two months that new employee knew our business inside out.

Of course, this route meant that all the SOPs have the same look and feel, which again improves clarity and comprehension.

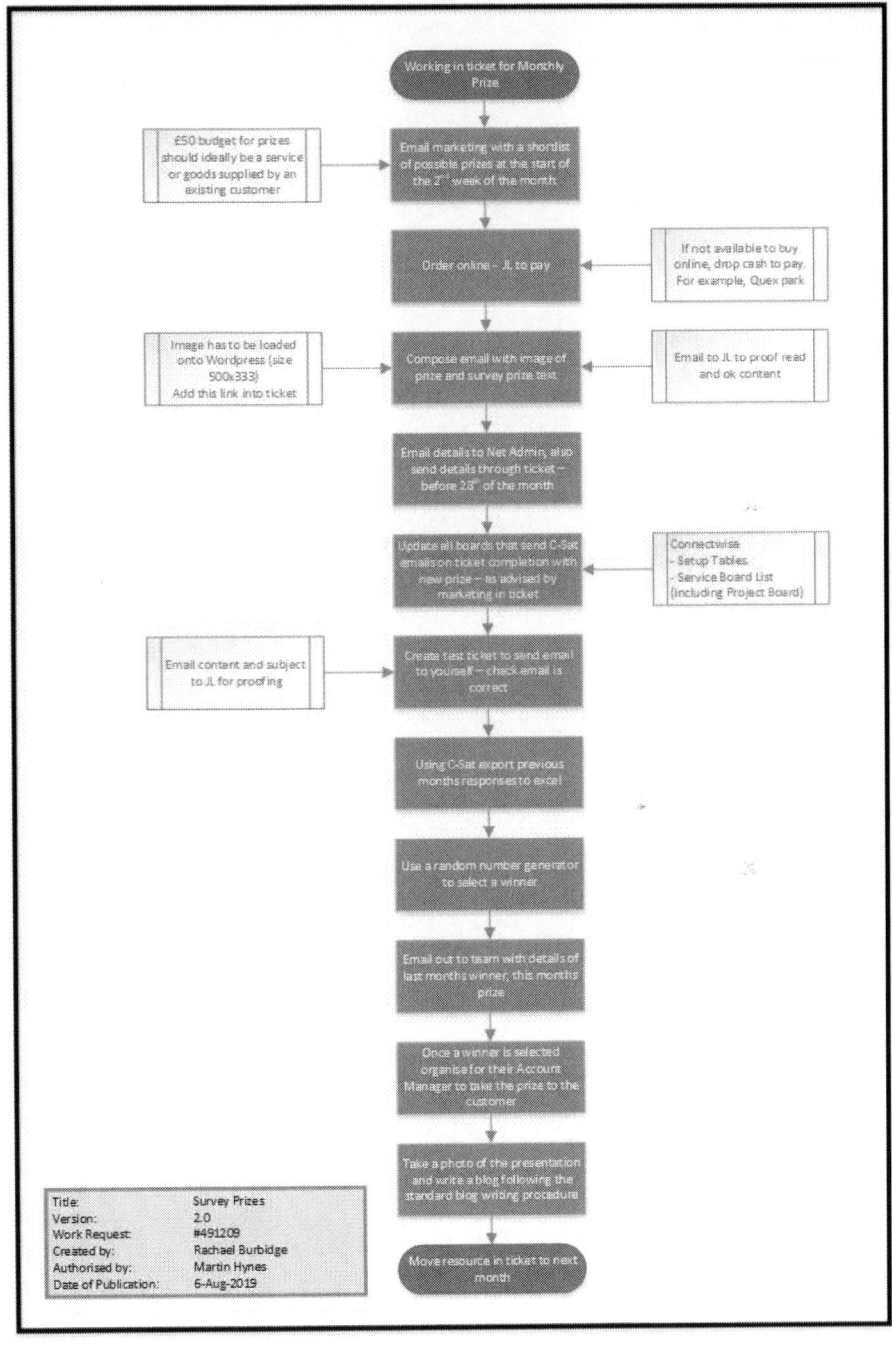

Working in ticket for Monthly Prize

£50 budget for prizes should ideally be a service or goods supplied by an existing customer → Email marketing with a shortlist of possible prizes at the start of the 2nd week of the month

Order online - JL to pay ← If not available to buy online, drop cash to pay. For example, Quex park

Image has to be loaded onto Wordpress (size 500x333) Add this link into ticket → Compose email with image of prize and survey prize text ← Email to JL to proof read and ok content

Email details to Net Admin, also send details through ticket – before 23rd of the month

Update all boards that send C-Sat emails on ticket completion with new prize – as advised by marketing in ticket ← Connectwise - Setup Tables - Service Board List (including Project Board)

Email content and subject to JL for proofing → Create test ticket to send email to yourself – check email is correct

Using C-Sat export previous months responses to excel

Use a random number generator to select a winner

Email out to team with details of last months winner, this months prize

Once a winner is selected organise for their Account Manager to take the prize to the customer

Take a photo of the presentation and write a blog following the standard blog writing procedure

Move resource in ticket to next month

Title:	Survey Prizes
Version:	2.0
Work Request:	#491209
Created by:	Rachael Burbidge
Authorised by:	Martin Hynes
Date of Publication:	6-Aug-2019

Stage Four – Map your employees

Naturally, I know you have been itching to do this. Look at who you have in your team today and where they best fit.

A few notes to help you in this process:

The first step is to assign the leaders of the teams. If you don't have people today who you think can do this role, don't assume to pick the best you have for the job. You are better off putting the Managing Directors name in those roles if that's today's truth. From there you can work on developing future leaders to allow you to hand over those functions.

Then assign the rest of your team. Unless you have added new roles that today you don't utilise you should have a name in every box.

In our example from earlier, Bob's employee Sue was working in all three functional areas, getting work, doing work and getting paid. Sue was stressed and overworked and Bob was thinking of getting an extra member of staff. When Bob maps his staff into his functional role-based organisation chart today, Sue will appear three times. She will have roles under each of these functional areas of the business. When the new colleague arrives, Sue will be relinquishing one of her roles to the new person. As such, at this point, it's not a problem for a member of your team to appear more than once, but there should be no dotted lines of functionality.

In our example, we had the purchasing and invoicing functions under one role. Should that role become too big for one person, we would split it into two roles, both reporting to the finance manager. You would just split the list of functions accordingly.

As you complete this process you will gain clarity of who you need to recruit or train as you grow your business.

Stage Five – Assign understudies for all roles

As we are making good progress here, the next step is to consider one massive 'what if'.

The challenge for most managing directors is relinquishing control. To yield power to the leadership team can make the managing director feel exposed. What happens for example if the person in the sales leader role leaves?

Now you have clarity of organisational structure the next step is to work out if within your team you have potential next-generation leaders. If you have, start developing them early. There are a couple of great reasons why you will want to do this.

Holiday and sickness cover coming from within the team means that the managing director can continue to work on strategy and vision.

Should one of your leaders have an extended period of absence or even leave the company, you have someone who could step up with minimum business interruption.

Stage Six - Share the completed diagram with your whole team

My experience is that people welcome clarity, but they don't like to be ambushed. Your new vision of organisational clarity may not match what your team believed. If every member of staff believed that they had a direct line to the managing director, introducing a team leader between them can feel like a demotion.

That doesn't change the truth, but it does change how you need to approach your announcement.

For most of your employees, this update is best handled at a companywide team meeting so you can answer any questions that may arise. However, think about any sensitive characters in your team who may feel slighted by your new structure and consider having a 1-2-1 meeting ahead of the team meeting.

I recommend you start by introducing the 3-to-5-year organisational chart as a picture of where you are heading. The team will be delighted to know you have a long-term plan.

Then explain the various functions and responsibility of those roles. By doing this, lots of the people who today have no responsibility for leading will have already realised that they are not in the leadership roles.

Introduce the leadership team and explain why you feel these people have the skills that the role and its responsibilities require whilst stressing the value of the people working within their teams. If as the managing director you are covering any of these key leadership roles, you can explain this is an interim stage whilst you recruit or train someone for the role.

Company-Wide – Corporate Image

The Why?

Many years ago, I was introduced to the saying 'World-class at getting ready'. Criticism of business owners who spent more time crafting their new company branding than they spent getting it out in front of prospects. Logic will tell you that a piece of marketing that is 95% good enough and in the post to your prospect has a better chance of working than hoping that one day it will be 100% good enough and it never leaving your desk.

And that's where the problems begin.

As your business grows you will need to empower your staff to send things out without a necessity for you to sign off on everything that leaves. Your definition of 95% good enough and your employee's definition may not be the same. The cause of this challenge is the lack of guidance as to what 100% perfect looks like.

Corporate image is not limited to just your choice of font or colour of shirts. It's a much wider topic than that. The areas we will cover in this chapter include:

- **Corporate Branding** – This is about your logo and how it can be used, your choice of colours and fonts.

- **Social Media** – You don't own your employee's accounts, but if you want them to promote your content how do you want that done so it comes from your corporate voice. What standard content should they have within their LinkedIn profile?

- **Political Views** – There are advantages of guiding what makes suitable posts on personal social media accounts.

- **Email Signatures** – Do you have a standard sign-off? Are employees allowed to modify this to suit their requirements?

- **Corporate Workwear** – Where and when should it be worn. Where should it not be worn?

- **Work from Home** – The mismatch between you and your employee's view of what is acceptable.

Method

The purpose of this chapter is to ask you to think about the various opportunities to create your brand, share your message and in many cases protect your image from damage.

Corporate Branding

When thinking about big brands such as Coca Cola, Carlsberg or Cadbury you can't picture a time when you didn't know of them. The logo, font and colour are embedded in your memory. The reason that has happened is that they are consistent in how they present their image to you. Take two steps back and look at how you present to the world. Is your logo design and colours the same on your office, vans, website, business cards, email signatures the same? What about the font used in correspondence? When did you last check what your team are sending out to make sure this is consistent?

Could you picture a Blue Coca-Cola image? Or Carlsberg being written in a Times New Roman.

You should consider having a plan to regularly review everything that goes out with your logo on and provide training and guidance to your team as required. Consider creating a 'Branding Guidelines' document.

Social Media

A missed opportunity for most of the businesses I know is the employees own social media presence. The question therefore is, if your team love their jobs why don't they share more of your content on social media? The answer is often because they don't have guidance as to what to post or why it matters. It is not made easy for them to help. If you have 10 staff and they all have 100 unique contacts on their social media, your new reach is potentially a further 1,000 opportunities to get your messages in front of a wider audience. Create regular content that is suitable for your team to share. Ensure you start this process by teaching your team why sharing content is good for them and their employer. Remember that your next employees could well be friends with your existing employees. Show this audience the happy and healthy workplace you have.

With a more business-like platform such as LinkedIn, I recommend you create a standardised image. Create a model of how you would like it to look and be used and provide guidance and support to help your team update their profiles.

You should provide guidance, complete with profile wallpaper images for your team to standardise their LinkedIn profile to show their corporate allegiance. Create a strategy to provide suitable content for your employees to post out on social media. The void caused by the absence of your guidance will generally result in chaos with each of your team creating their 'standard'.

Political Views

I mentioned the value of your team's social media accounts, but employee's political views posts merit some discussion. Often business owners have said to me about their employee's accounts, "It's their profile, so it's up to them what they post". The issue here is of course that their views, when shared on social media platforms, can harm your business and therefore by extension, their livelihoods.

You can be sure that when one of your employee's posts that contain racist, homophobic or xenophobic content is noticed, they will also notice the name of their employer! This makes it your problem and so it's worth considering what steps you can take to avoid this reputation damage.

In some respects, this one is easy to fix as it's just about making your employees aware and providing training as required. It's worth doing pre-emptively. I worked for a large company that did this with online training, but you could also workshop it at a team all-up meeting. Help them understand what makes acceptable and not acceptable posts in our new more feelings aware communication environment. Teach them to see their communication from the perspective of others.

Email Signatures

There are two parts to this. The law and the opportunity.

- **The Law** - The UK Companies Act states that your company email footers need to include your registered company name, company registration number and place of registration. Many businesses fail to do this correctly, allowing staff to tack whatever message they want at the end of the emails they send. Or often, adding nothing.

- **The Opportunity** – I read an article that said that the average company employee sent 40 emails per day in 2020. That's 40 opportunities to show the recipients your professionalism, plus with the subtle addition of a link to some valuable content or call-to-action. Of course, your signature should always have a way for the recipient to opt-out of the email tennis with other ways to contact you like phone numbers.

Review how your new emails and replies are signed off. Consider installing some email signature software that will allow you to standardise and make your emails more consistent and remove the need for the employees to manually add them. Create some lead bait to valuable content on your website as support for your marketing activity.

Corporate Workwear

I am a massive fan of corporate workwear, even in our post-pandemic mostly work-from-home environment. Again, like all the other branding topics it needs to be consistent. Add to this the need for it to be clean and replaced at least as often as you would replace your regular work clothes. Giving each employee just two poor grade printed T-Shirts won't address the need to create a smart image.

- **Advertising and Brand Awareness** – First and foremost this is about nailing your colours to the mast. A way of showing the world that you are here to do business. It's another great way to get your branding in front of people.

- **Customer reassurance** – When your team introduce themselves to your customers, they know they are from your company. This is especially important in a business-to-consumer environment but professional in business-to-business too.

- **Worn with pride** – Assuming your team like the uniform you have selected they will wear it consistently. It's kind of easier in the morning to pull on the corporate workwear than it is to think about what they need to wear. Any supplied uniform needs to be appropriate for the working environment. For example, warehouse workers need layers suitable for all seasons. Uniform helps the feeling of being connected to their work family. Their tribe.

- **Health & safety** – Depending on your work environment it's useful to quickly identify the people from your organisation both for customers and colleagues. In the case of environments where you need your team to wear personal protective clothing, this too can be branded. My organisation didn't do much 'construction site' work, but when they did the staff had branded high visibility jackets.

- **When should it not be worn?** – Assuming you don't make your branded uniform merchandise that you sell, it is a safe assumption that everyone who is wearing your brand works for your company. Your current staff should see why everything they do in uniform impacts the brand. When someone leaves your employment request the uniform back for recycling to avoid it being used for the council refuse site run.

Consider investing in corporate workwear. Bring a small team of employees together to research what would work for your team. Don't scrimp on quality or quantity when it comes to uniform. Your plan needs to include how quickly you intend to get uniform for new starters and how quickly you plan to refresh any worn-out items.

Work from Home

Following on from the topic of corporate workwear leads us directly to the need to have a definition of what's acceptable when it comes to working from home when participating in video calls.

- **Workwear** – Do your staff need to wear their corporate image when working from home and attending video calls? If not, are slogan t-shirts acceptable? If you don't define the rules, staff will decide for themselves.

- **Lighting** – How many calls have you participated in where the person you are speaking with is in silhouette with the window behind them? If you don't want your staff to look like they are in a witness protection programme, check their environment and guide any required improvement.

- **Background** – Most video conference software can provide a blurred background which is infinitely better than seeing a pile of clothes waiting to be ironed. What are your employees sharing about their home life?

- **Privacy** – Your duty to keep your data confidential includes any processes that allow your staff to work from home. Is your data still safe and hidden from prying eyes?

Company-Wide - Products & Services Offering

The Why?

Part one – Review the number of products and services you offer today?

How many products and services do you currently offer to your customers? You may want to simplify and thus strengthen this area of your operation for the following reasons:

1. **Confused customers don't spend** - Too many offerings will confuse the customers into inactivity. If deciding is too hard, they will defer making the decision.

2. **Are you a generalist?** - It's just not possible to be a specialist in everything, so if you have too many offerings, you will become and be seen by your customers as a generalist.

3. **Profitability** - Specialists are generally more profitable than generalists, assuming you are a specialist in the right things and they are things your customers want to buy.

4. **Mind the Gap** - Maintaining the required skills and accreditations within your business is easier with a narrow scope of offerings. When you bring new people into your company it's easier to close the skills gap if you have an achievable training plan.

Part Two – A process to add new products and service offerings.

How can you safely add new product and service offerings without rushing them in because of a perceived need for one customer or prospect?

With the work completed in Part one, you will now also always want to consider if a new product will be added or whether it will become a replacement of something within your current offering.

If it is a replacement, what is the process to move your customers to your new offering?

Method

Mature businesses have a very defined 'stack' of products. For clarity here, a packaged and priced service is also called a 'product'. Less mature businesses tend to be happy to sell anything to anyone that wants to buy and have a less fixed view of what is in their product stack. The goal of this process is to narrow down your sales scope to no more than three products in any group.

Part One – Remove the confusion

The first stage of this is to work out what you sell today. Go back through your invoices and make a list of what you have sold and how much of your revenue comes from this product. Depending on your sector this could be brands of stairlift, computer systems or double-glazed windows. Make it a meaningful representative set of your data, even if that means going back 12 months. Group similar products together.

From each group, you need to look at the top three products by sales volume (how many you have sold) and sales revenue (how much you invoiced out). Then show the gross margin you retained from these sales (selling price minus the materials and direct labour costs) and what that represents as a percentage of your sales revenue. Although you may have many products in each group, there will be no major compelling reason to look further than the top three at this point.

The next step is to record any current accreditations you hold to sell and support these products. Include details of how many of your team have been trained in these products. Then finally, and you may need to speak to your suppliers, but find out if there are any market development, training incentives or volume bonuses available should you place more of your business with them.

Product Group	Vendor	Sales Volume	Sales Revenue	Gross Margin	Gross Margin %	Accreditations	Vendor Incentives
Stairlift	Sapphire	15	£150K	£40K	27%	Sales & Engineer Training.	Additional 5% discount at £200K revenue
Stairlift	Gamma	20	£120K	£20K	17%	No qualifications	No incentives
Stairlift	Rapid Lift	12	£108K	£25K	23%	Engineer training	5% rebate for marketing

With this data collected, you can start to analyse the table and make some observations as I have from the supplied example data.

- Sapphire – The highest contributor to sales revenue, with the greatest unit sale price at £10K and highest gross margin percentage.
- Gamma - Least profitable with the lowest unit sale price at £6K, the least accreditations and the least dealer support for the businesses continued growth plans.
- Rapid Lift – Third place for sales revenue, but second place for contribution to gross margin. A unit price of £9K.

Once you have made your observations, you can move to make recommendations, which again mine follow:

The Sapphire relationship should be nurtured. As you are selling a total of £378K of lifts today, it is worth going back and asking for a further target incentive rather than just the existing £200K target. Maybe if they can't give further margin, see if they can provide you with some marketing support.

Gamma is a cheap product creating a low gross margin percentage so you should look to remove this from your product stack. Investigate how many of these orders could have been upsold to the higher quality Sapphire product. If you could have moved 8 of these sales (40%) you will have achieved the same contribution to gross margin. If your business operating costs are running at 20% and you are only making 17% on this product line, you know you need to resolve this situation. The chapter on Financial Control will provide more guidance on this.

The Rapid Lift product price point should mean that the business could be moved over to the Sapphire product easily making an additional 4% margin on all sales upfront. The beneficial impact of this would be that you would reach the vendor incentive for an additional 5% margin and perhaps any greater negotiated margin.

When you complete your analysis, you may also want to factor in the remedial and support costs and your customer feedback. As in, if Rapid Lift has better customer service and produces happier customers, maybe that's the brand you focus your attention on as you reduce the number of options in your product stack.

Your next step would be to repeat this process for all your products and create a plan to cover any training gaps for your team to be able to sell, install and support this reduced product stack.

Lastly, there is sometimes a justification for having a low cost and a premium product in each sector but from experience, this makes your marketing message very difficult.

I used to strongly believe in the Bronze, Silver and Gold pricing model. Or Good, Better & Best. The idea being that you never want to sell the 'Bronze' offering, but it's priced to attract prospects. You then try and upsell them to the 'Silver' or even 'Gold' offering. Two things changed my view on this.

Our team hated servicing the low cost 'Bronze' offering. The reduced quality meant a greater level of remedial attention was needed. Of course, it also meant we were attracting customers with no money.

One of my long-term customers described this sales method as 'The Bronze Scam' and I guess I kind of felt like I had been found out. Instead of being confident in my product offering I was trying to use sales tactics rather than emotional educated reasoning. My business was better than that. I am better than that. I just needed to be confident.

This is a very old piece of theory but there is a saying that customers want their products to be cheap (price), great (quality) and fast (service) but they need to pick which two of those are more important which will be at the expense of the third one.

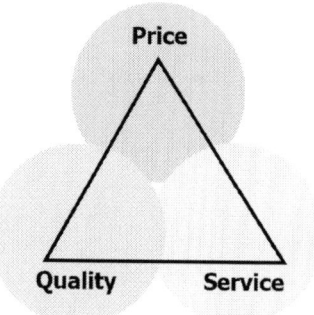

- Low price and great service will be at the expense of product quality.
- Low price and great quality product will be at the expense of the service that you can provide.

If you think that you will gain your business growth from being great at service and supplying a quality product and there is an available market to serve, now is the time to realise that you also need to be price confident. Ditch your 'Bronze' priced offering.

With that said, I am not saying there is not a place for a Silver and Gold offering. Or perhaps Standard and Premium. The difference is that your standard offering becomes the one you go to market with and that you are happy to sell every day. If a customer has more money in their budget you can offer them a premium option. It is understood that 20% of your customers will buy a premium offering – but only if you have one to sell them.

Part Two – Add new products using a repeatable process

Having put the work in on reducing your product stack, you don't want to be randomly adding new products back without having given them sufficient scrutiny. There are three reasons you may wish to add new products to your stack.

- **New Market** - You don't currently have any products in this product group and this is a new business area where you are looking to become active. Your process is going to be used to try and identify all the risks of entering this new market. What is the problem you are going to solve and why will you and your business be good at this?

- **Replacement** - You want to replace an existing product in your stack. Why have you fallen out of love with your existing product and why will this new one be better for your customer's experience and your business success? How easy will it be to move your customers over to this new product? What is the real total cost to make the switch and how long will it take to recover these costs? When you are evaluating the product consider if your new product has different functionality and the impact that may have on some of your existing customers whom you plan to switch to your new offering.

- **Additional** - This one creates questions such as what this additional product provides that your existing product doesn't. Where does it fit strategically for your business? Is this a lower cost or higher quality offering? Again, you need to get to the real total cost of adding this product.

In all cases, you want to ask questions such as how long it will take to recover the costs for your investment in equipment and training before you can make a profit. And of course, what would be the impact of this product rollout not happening as per plan and you therefore never making a profit?

The following questions will help you make a start, but add whatever is specific to your business sector.

- **Product and Market?** - Is this a product for a new market, a replacement product or an additional product? Name of the product including vendor if applicable. Alternatives considered? What does it do? Why is this good for the client? How does it work?

- **How can you sell it?** - Pricing mechanisms, limits, assumptions & caveats. Are there sales battle cards & marketing collateral available? Need for technical sales training? Who are the competitors for this product?

- **How do you set it up?** - Pre-installation questions. Installation method. Documentation required, ahead of installation as well as after installation

- **What are the costs and expected return?** – Internal labour cost to investigate this solution and to get this product into the stack including demonstration equipment, tooling and internal training. Ongoing annual support and maintenance costs. Timescale before you can sell this for the first time. What do you predict is the market size and sales level and gross margin you expect in the next 12 months?

- **How do you financially control it?** – Will the sales and purchase invoicing frequency be in alignment with existing products? What detail is required for customers? How can you control costs including labour measurement to the true cost of product tracked to enable gross margin calculations?

- **Who owns this product?** - Who owns this product within your team and who are the internal stakeholders who will contribute to the discussion? Who will review and approve this product? Which customers could be the early adopters providing feedback?

- **What are the risks?** - Of delivering this product (time, money, liability). And of NOT delivering this Product (customer retention, competitive advantage)?

You need a solid evaluation process for the following reasons:

- **Avoid Confusion** - Lack of internal process could mean that your choice of product and service offering just ends up confused again and you are back to where you were before you became a specialist.

- **Rejection Risks** – With a desire to keep your products and services catalogue short, you mustn't reject new ideas without considering the value they could bring. You need a process so you know how to review and score the opportunity.

- **Costs Analysis** – You need to know how much it will cost before you can start to sell the new product or service including allocating the budget for vendor training, initial tooling and equipment set-up costs. Ensure you take advantage of any accreditation programme or available market development funds or grant funding.

- **Commercial Viability** - Your process here will help you apply your pricing strategy to the offering and check that the commercial elements of the offering work for you. There is normally no point in taking on a new offering if you will make a loss by selling it.

- **Size of Opportunity** – You may have a request to make your product in a new colour, but having this process will help you understand if that colour is saleable to enough of the market you serve to justify the investment in starting production in that new colour.

- **Opportunity Cost** - Doing something may mean not doing something else. As in, there will be a limit to how many new products or services you can create this year within your finite resource. Pick the ones that will drive your business, in alignment with your completed foundation plan.

- **Ownership** – There is an amount of work required to evaluate a new opportunity and someone on your team must be taking responsibility for the steps that could lead to you making important decisions, especially the timing for this process.

Company-Wide - Next Big Thing

The Why?

What your customer needs and what you provide today may not be what your customer needs tomorrow and therefore what you need to be ready to provide. The chances are that this need to adapt will happen to you rather than be caused by you. Your market will be disrupted and although quite blunt, you need to be ready to evolve or face extinction.

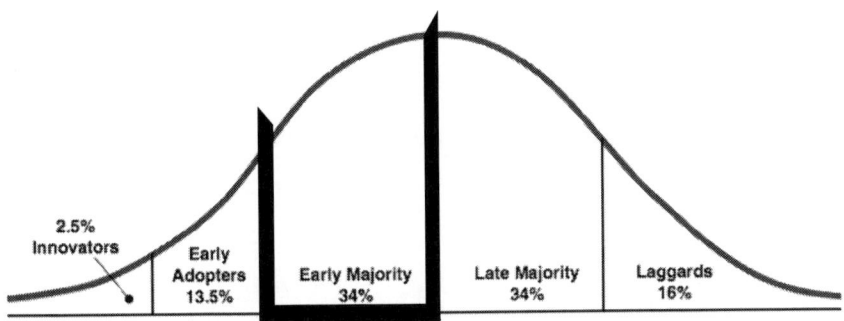

I would like to introduce you to a product lifecycle standard deviation bell curve, charting the normal expected life of a product. For clarity, the term product includes packaged and priced service offerings.

There are two parts to this chapter. The first is that although you don't need to be the innovator in your sector, you do need to ensure you have a plan to keep sight of the next big thing that you should be getting ready to supply to take advantage of the profitable early majority.

The second part is to ensure that you know when you have tipped over into the late majority. Left unchecked, that slope to the bottom will lead to your commoditised business offerings becoming irrelevant in your marketplace. You need to know when to leap to your next big thing.

Method

To help with gaining a common understanding, please find the following definitions of the stages across the bell curve on the previous page.

- **Innovators** – These customers will buy whatever you have to sell them at almost any price. Sadly, there just are not enough customers in this group to build your business upon. Your unit costs are very high in this section as you need to recover your research investment.

- **Early Adopters** – With some education available to your prospects and once there are a few Google reviews to satisfy their need for research, these customers will leap to buy your new offering and again, they are profitable but there are just not enough of them.

- **Early Majority** – For this part of the graph you have named your price, the market wants what you sell and there are not too many competitors vying for the market. Whilst serving these customers you will work on reducing your costs and optimising your supply, making this the most profitable section of the sales cycle.

- **Late Majority** – As per the graph, it's all downhill from here. At this point, the barrier to entry is lower and competitors don't need to educate the prospects to the value being proposed. New competitors will appear and their main point of difference will be that they are cheaper than you. For a while, you will defend that by saying 'but we are better' before you realise that it's not your opinion that matters here. Your customers in this section don't hear your protestations.

- **Laggards** – This group are only buying because they reluctantly must. There is very little profit or customer satisfaction in this section of the available market.

A great mentor of mine described the journey as you shoot down the slope servicing the late majority and the laggards as your business offering becoming 'irrelevant'. The last thing you want to do is wake to find what you do and the market you serve has moved on and you didn't.

With that said, the other place you may not want to be positioning your business is at the front of the bell curve. Or the bleeding edge, as it is sometimes known.

For every great new idea that you have heard of, there are probably thousands that never made it to the public domain. Somebody somewhere will always be spending a fortune to create new products, in the hope that it is the next big thing.

Now of course if you are in pharmaceuticals and hoping to come up with the next vaccine that you plan to patent and retain all manufacturing rights, this model doesn't work. But for most readers of this book, second place is not a losing position in the race to innovate your business. Consider the next big thing as a parallel to the life of a gazelle. To avoid becoming lion food you don't need to be the fastest gazelle, just not the slowest.

Ideally, you want to join the market at about halfway through the early adopters so there is a proven demand thus reducing your risk and you will have become good at supplying your product by the time the early majority start buying. You then need to be ready to get back out and onto the next big thing as the late majority start buying.

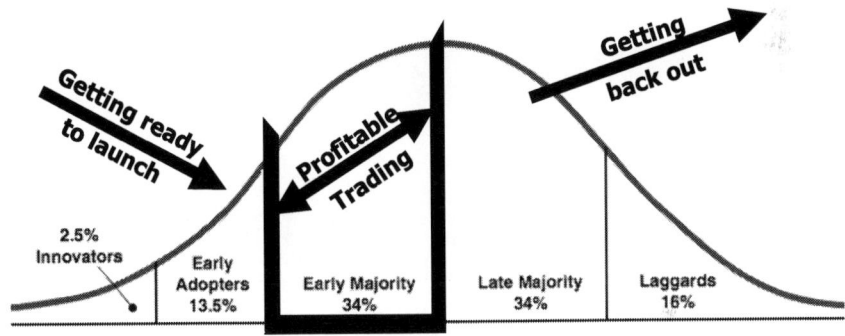

Part One – Keeping your eyes open

It's not normally a problem that you will not be servicing the innovators at the front of the curve, but you need to be very ready to service them before the early majority phase starts buying but how will you know what is going to be the next big thing? Getting the timing right is critical, so these two steps are worth following.

Open-Minded

You need to be open to there being better ways to do what you do today. This is often difficult to do because you have invested so much in your current operation from defining and pricing your product, through tools and training of your team to educating and selling it to your customers. In a perfect world, you would like what you sell today to continue forever without any new competitors coming in with better or cheaper products. Sadly, that perfect world doesn't exist.

Inquisitive

To find out what the customers who are known as 'innovators' are buying and who from, you need to spend time with them and think like an innovator. You need to visit the same 'watering holes' and enjoy some of the same experiences. Connect with them on social platforms. Who writes about your sector? Are you reading what they write?

Who are the people in your sector who have an authoritative voice? Follow them and read what they publish. If you find that two out of the three you follow are talking about the same product and you don't offer it to your customers today, you may have just found your next big thing.

Part Two – Spotting the signs

There is no warning as you approach the top of the hill on the product lifecycle bell curve.

The first you will know is as you are heading down the hill on the other side.

So how will you know you have stepped over from the early majority to the late majority?

Here are some signs you can watch out for.

Although your existing customers came to you for your quality and service, your competitors' approach with a price-based proposition is starting to cause increased attrition. Initially, you think that your competitors are mad for offering their services at such a low price, until you realise that they have managed to deliver at scale, in ways you didn't innovate to achieve.

The new prospects you are speaking with have a lower maturity in all aspects of their business. Remember, as you trip over the top of the curve, the most forward-thinking 50% of the available business has already bought this product. The late majority are only buying for fear of missing out or necessity. These new buyers tend not to value the quality and service in the same way that the first 50% insisted upon and are much more price-conscious.

As you approached the top of the curve, you were optimising your delivery and improving your profitability. As you go over into the late majority the pricing pressure will drive your gross profit margin down.

The method of delivering your product is widely understood and easy to replicate and as such, with a general lower barrier to entry, new competitors start to appear. Their operations are created in an optimised way so without the burden of history, they will continue to make bold promises at cheap prices that are designed to attract the late majority.

It is always worth periodically reviewing the root cause of your customer attrition and the reasons why you have not been winning recent sales orders for each of your products.

Company-Wide – Employee Wellbeing

The Why?

I am task-focussed to a fault (rather than being people focussed) and could never be accused of being politically correct. That said, this section matters to the future success of your business, so avoid it at your peril. I know this may come over as potentially insincere, but if you are in any way like me, you will do better at caring personally for your employees as real people if you start with a process to follow.

Let's start here with the Oxford dictionary definition of Wellbeing which reveals:

> *The state of being or doing well in life; happy, healthy, or prosperous condition; moral or physical welfare (of a person or community).*

From this, you can see that wellbeing is a very broad topic and any processes created will be equally broad. You are aiming for a holistic person focussed view of workplace wellbeing.

Within this book, I address the need for regular employee meetings and equitable pay structures. In addition to those two, you will also typically want to consider having a plan for at least the following ten points:

1. Measure employee satisfaction with a clear commitment to resolving issues.
2. Helping employees connect to and communicate with each other.
3. Physical activities that are both for teams and individuals.
4. Ensuring rewards and incentive programmes match the employee's needs.
5. Social events put on by the employees for the employees.
6. Helping employees learn new skills.
7. Community engagement opportunities.
8. Mental health support and the ability to connect with appropriate resources.
9. A mechanism to allow the voice of your employees to be heard.
10. Ensuring inclusion.

Improving employee wellbeing is proven to reduce employee turnover, reduce absenteeism, improve happiness and relationships, improve performance, enhance physical health and reduce workplace stress.

For you, as the business owner, it creates an environment that can make the business more profitable and easier to recruit for your growing workforce.

Method

This one is a big and very important topic. As I said at the start of this chapter, not everyone is wired in a way that means they are always thinking about others. The great news is that you can and almost certainly will learn to achieve this skill as you mature as a business leader. Until you can do this naturally and without thinking, I would like you to consider creating these ten processes for your business.

The one topic I have not mentioned here is communication. Your effective communication contributes to wellness and I will cover that in the next chapter.

1. Measure employee satisfaction with a clear commitment to resolving issues

If you are not doing it yet, once you have read the rest of this book, you and your leadership team will be meeting with all employees weekly. These meetings are a great opportunity to develop and support the employees on an individual basis. As such, this process is not about any individual's view of their happiness.

To gain any kind of meaningful feedback from your employees, they would need to believe it is safe that they can tell you how they feel without fear of recrimination. If you have not been the most approachable leader to date, this is something that will take time to achieve.

There are plenty of anonymous internet-based platforms that will ask weekly questions to measure employee satisfaction. Take a look at www.tinypulse.com as an example provider.

Because as a 'pulse' they will ask the monthly question "How happy are you at work", in time you can measure whether your team is becoming happier or less happy. Remember, happiness is subjective. As a leader, when you hear that your team are averagely only 6 out of 10 happy, you can't help but feel you have let them down or even worse write off their opinions as being wrong!

During the other weeks, the platform can ask other questions. You can normally also insert your questions if required. If you ask the question "Rate the choice of coffee and snacks in the break room?", and then include the open question, "What would make it better?" which will therefore engage your team in the process of improvement.

Depending on what is going on in an individual's life will determine how they answer the question. My recommendation is that you make your focus for any actions from this measuring process for the whole team rather than trying to make any individual happier.

If you have 15 staff and 1 of them scores their happiness as 2 out of 10 your instinct is to find out who that person is so you can dismiss their opinion as being an 'outlier' that can be ignored because they are messing with the data you wanted to read. The mature leader will realise that they need to try even harder to connect with the whole team.

The magic of employee satisfaction for the employees doesn't come from you measuring it, but from you making a difference to their working lives because you are listening and acting on their feedback. Therefore, it goes almost without saying, asking for feedback and then ignoring it will put you in a worse position than you started. As such, don't just fix things quietly in the background, but remember to shout about all the success stories.

Create or buy into a system to get an anonymous pulse of employee happiness and a plan to review and act on the suggestions given.

2. Helping employees connect to and communicate with each other

As teams grow, so naturally does the creation of potentially damaging cliques. Subgroups with their agendas. It is not the presence of the group that is damaging, but the risk that they may cause a feeling of exclusion. Often this will be more psychological than just that people who are left out are truly missing out. Well-being is very much about the whole person.

You can't stop the cliques, but you can make them the secondary way of communicating. As in, make it easier for your team to communicate through the 'approved channel' than to go off and create their own. Depending on your sector, this could be private Facebook groups, WhatsApp groups, Microsoft Teams, Slack channels or just an old school email distribution group.

Back in the day, my business which had no more than 30 employees at any point, introduced a social@ email group. That was the place to send jokes, social invites, event details etc. They have since moved to a Microsoft Teams based solution, but the principals continue. Importantly this is an inclusive club. Everyone is welcome.

If you don't yet have a standard, choose a company social communication platform. Work with your employees to see what the most popular choice is. Add it to your onboarding process for new employees and put it in the handbook. Then encourage some of your best social connector employees to drive its adoption across the team.

3. Physical activities that are both for teams and individuals

I have never been fanatically committed to team sports but for some people, they can't picture a world without their football – playing or just watching. Some of your team however may find playing a game of chess energetic. Physical activities are about balance.

When you come to introducing events to your team you need to factor in the general appetite and again, ensure you are not excluding anyone from everything you put on. By this, I mean that if you have some of your team who love to go bowling, but hate to play football, don't make all your events around football.

Examples of events for individuals could include walking step-count challenges or weight loss challenges. To support these activities, you can share walking routes or diet tips to provide support to the participants.

Team or family events could be active sports like football, paintball or cycling challenges. And less active events could include bowling or walking treasure hunts but where you can, outside is always best when it comes to wellbeing.

Consider introducing some regular challenges that have a physical element to them. An opportunity for people to work either as teams with their colleagues, as individuals or even as their family groups. Look to engage one of the team to own the event but support them fully to ensure it's successful.

4. Ensuring rewards and incentive programmes match the employees needs or wants

Understanding your team's needs help you create incentive programmes that motivate your team to achieve. Getting it wrong isn't just a lack of incentives, but a scheme that actively disincentivises the behaviours you are looking to create.

Often salespeople are described as 'coin operated' meaning that they can be motivated easily by money, but it would be a mistake to assume that works for everyone.

Abraham Maslow's hierarchy of needs in 1943, defined human motivation. His paper talks about the idea that the needs build on each other in a specific order.

The joke here is that having a fast internet connection

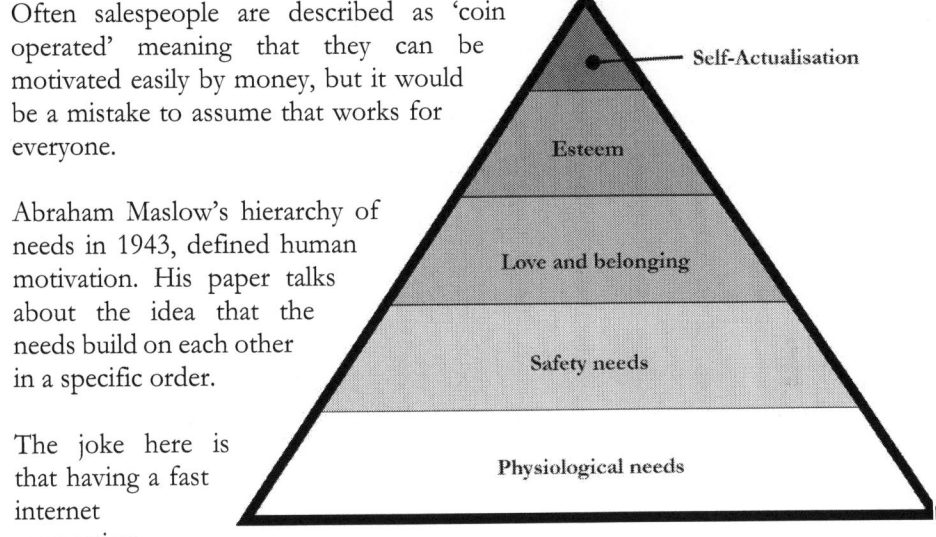

should be added to this list as part of the physiological needs. Strangely Maslow didn't think this to be important in 1943.

- **Physiological needs** - The idea was that until a person has their physiological needs met (air, water, food, shelter, sleep, clothing, reproduction).
- **Safety needs** - Once they have that covered, they start to look at keeping their physiological needs met in the future. Investments of time and money at this point include health, property and job security.
- **Love and belonging** – With some stability, we can then look to improve our connection with the tribe we belong to. Friendship, intimacy and family connections.
- **Esteem** – At this point, we are looking to have our input recognised and to be given more autonomy. Respect and status matters here.
- **Self-actualisation** – Now they have nothing to prove to others, this final phase is where a person's purpose is to become the best version of themselves.

There was little science behind his theory, but the one takeaway that exists in most studies is that once the physiological needs are met, all the other sections become important. And how important will depend on the individual's mindset and circumstances.

Until your team are earning sufficiently well to take care of their psychological needs, don't think about any incentive schemes. Just help your team work hard enough to earn well enough.

Following that and as part of the one-to-one sessions, you and your leadership team have with your team, find out what matters to them. It's as simple as having an open dialogue. For some, they value time with their families more than money. For example, these incentives map closely with Maslow's hierarchy of needs.

- More money in their pay packet.
- Health insurance and pensions
- Time off to spend with the family.
- Greater authority in the workplace
- Opportunity to help their community interest.

Once you know what your employees need, it's easier to create a scheme. If your employee achieves targets, that are within their control, you can reward them with something meaningful. Talk with them and ascertain what motivates each of your team. Define what they could do to drive your business forward that in return would allow you to help them achieve their goals.

5. Social events put on by the employees for the employees

I kind of touched on this regarding the physical activities in number 3, but the important bit here is to get the team themselves to arrange their events. The business needs to pay or contribute to the events to make them happen, but attendance will be driven by the team's ownership.

In my previous business, we made an allowance of £30 per quarter per employee to allow for events. If they chose to just go for a meal at the local all you can eat Chinese restaurant, our company contribution would pay the whole bill. If they chose go-karting, the £30 per employee would perhaps pay half of the bill.

Our success came from making these quarterly events, set a year in advance. Some employees are much better than others in the 'Social Secretary' role, but it's important to try and share this role out. Your guidance should also include teaching your employee team member 'volunteers' what makes an inclusive event, to stop all the year's events from being of no interest to half of the workforce.

As the managing director, I only ever attended as 'one of the lads'. I didn't do too badly at the ten-pin bowling, was part of the winning team at the Escape Room and always lost miserably at the karting, much to my embarrassment as I owned one of the fastest cars in the car park and the team made sure I knew it!

A word of warning about team building.

I was working with a team leader of a company who said to me *"The management are putting weekend team-building events on and most of the staff are not attending. What can we do to insist they attend these weekend events?"*

My opinion here is that team building should be an outcome and not the primary objective of any planned event. The team that plays together, stays together. Your role as a leader is to empower, stimulate and pay for environments where relationships can blossom. At the point you tell people it's team building, the value of these events has all but gone! Keep the value of these social events as a benefit or perk of working for such an amazing company.

Do you think you can create a budget to subsidise social events? Which of your employees do you think could be approached and asked to arrange a social event for the whole team? Get one event in the diary and see if there is an appetite to schedule regular events.

6. Helping employees learn new skills

When I was a lad, you wouldn't start a car repair task without a trusty Haines manual in your hand. Now for pretty much every task, you could undertake you can watch a YouTube video and learn all about it before you even lift the bonnet. In fact, for most tasks in life, you can generally muddle through using Google as your friend when you get stuck.

For clarification here, learning new skills is not always about gaining qualifications, but always leads to gaining more confidence. The sense of achievement is a massive boost to personal morale. The best companies used the time of the 2020 pandemic to help their employees focus on skill development and personal development. Not all skills desired will be directly related to the employees' current job role but will impact their emotional wellbeing and that's a good enough reason to have the conversation.

From the most recent one-to-one meetings that you and your leadership team have had with the employees, what are their learning goals? What can the company do to help them achieve?

7. Community engagement opportunities

Back to Maslow's hierarchy of needs, Love and belonging, Esteem & Self-actualisation are very much about a person's connections with the wider world.

Employees at my previous IT business could spend up to five fully paid days per year helping local community projects. Some walked retired greyhounds, helped older people use IT more effectively, inspired our next generation in schools or gave advice to business start-ups. As you can see, some wanted to utilise what they know to help others, but one just wanted to do something unrelated to work. Time out from their day job. What they all had in common though was a desire to put back into society.

I know this chapter is feeling like it's all about giving and a cost to the business but done well, each of the events listed above created positive discussions within the office and of course, social media activity that paints the business in a great light to all customers and prospects. Not all employees took advantage of this opportunity to serve others, but they were also not all at the same point in Maslow's hierarchy of needs.

Could you allow your team to invest company time in community engagement projects? Consider asking your employees what local projects they wish the company could support.

8. Mental health support and the ability to connect with appropriate resources

You are probably now saying 'Yeah, yeah. I know. Everyone is talking about mental health and I have heard it already'. But there is still a stigma. There is a massive step required for a person to make an appointment to visit the doctors and admit that they can't cope with their life. They need to do this to gain access to medication and a referral for a few hours of counselling.

Now counselling is almost certainly better than starting on what is likely to be regular medication. As you and your leadership team meet with your employees weekly, you are likely to be able to have caring authentic conversations and be aware when things are getting too much. I have known companies provide counselling services for their teams as a discussed benefit, albeit a benefit you hope the team will never need to utilise. Once the counsellors have spent some time with your employee, the next steps may be to refer them to the medical professionals, but you have lowered the barrier for getting help. You have made it safe.

Could you make a provision of access to counselling resources for your employees? And if you do, would you be willing to openly discuss this availability making it easier for your team to take the step to gain the help they need?

9. A mechanism to allow the voice of your employees to be heard

Everything you do WITH your employees has a greater chance of success than the things you do FOR, or even worse, TO your employees. By this I mean, if you can engage and involve your employees in any proposed changes, you already have their buy into it being successful.

Left unchecked, businesses can create a them-and-us situation with a feeling that the top tier management is making all the decisions and taking the glory and spoils of success where the workers at the bottom of the tree are working hard just to stand still from day to day. Within this section, I would like to introduce you to the role of an employee council, whose purpose is to provide a bridging mechanism between these two factions.

The employee council is a democratically elected body that will attend important strategic meetings of the business to bring the views of the workforce. They will also help disseminate the outcomes of these meetings to the workers. Does this all sound too big for your business today? I believe by the time you have 10 staff, it's worth having one of the workers at your top table. It keeps you honest in all your dealings.

Ultimately it is of course up to you whether you give your employee council president a vote, but my view is that if just one vote on top of you and your leadership teams votes tips the decision in favour of the staff it was probably the right outcome.

To create your employee council first work out a structure. For larger businesses, you may need to allow one employee representative from each department.

It could be that you have three large groups of people. Let's call them sales, installers and the admin group.

Explain the role of the council to the staff and invite expressions of interest to help the business at this level.

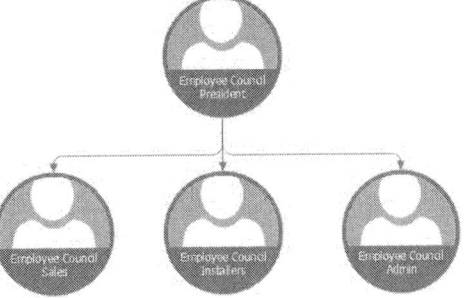

Encourage some competition and get lots of people to put themselves forward, so you can have an election. Make that bit fun and ideally a social occasion. Don't forget to celebrate the winners of these positions.

If you have multiple people on your employee council, run a second round of voting to decide the employee council president. This is the person that will attend the leadership meetings for the next couple of years until you run a new round of elections.

Lastly as a word of warning. The early days of your employee council will feature many operational discussions about 'tea and toilets'. As the process matures, so will the level of input that your employee council can bring to your strategic meetings. The more you engage the employee council, the better the value it will bring to your success.

10. Ensuring inclusion

Having worked through the last nine points in this chapter there is something for everyone in this plan to focus on your employee wellbeing. But what happens if people just don't want to engage with the things you are doing to help them?

Firstly, there are a couple of easy things you can do to reach the employees that won't feel like you are overstepping the mark.

- **Birthdays** – I always feel that when a quiet member of the team says it was my birthday yesterday, we have somehow let them down. Not everyone wants a big party, but a happy birthday from a colleague is never out of place. Create a way to celebrate birthdays in the workplace.

- **Anniversaries** – What do you do today to mark the occasion of the first, fifth and tenth work anniversaries? Remember, celebrating these events also helps the rest of the team to see how much you value their commitment to the business and team. In my last job, on the first anniversary, I was given an etched drinking cup and a certificate. Small costs and big impacts. I have just heard that my old company have started making a big deal of fifth anniversaries with things like the gifts of family weekend breaks.

Everyone in your team will have a birthday and anniversary. Celebrate with them.

If you or your leadership team are concerned that you have any team members who are not engaging, you will be able to safely discuss this with them at your weekly one-to-one meetings. With the safe environment, you have created you can gently learn what is making them feel disconnected.

Within this book, I can't give prescriptive advice as to what you can do to 'make it better' because it will be individual to the circumstances, but what I can tell you is that you can't do too much to make people feel valued. Investment in your employees on a personal level, which includes their families, will repay you in business success.

Start by diarising the birthdays and work anniversaries of all employees and as a leadership team decide how you can help mark these occasions.

Company-Wide - Communication

The Why?

How much is too much communication?

Holding the attention of the audience for your message is a skill. A person's attention span or time they can concentrate before becoming distracted is finite. Just think about your experience with YouTube adverts. If they can't hook you in before the 'Skip' button appears, you are gone and on to the next thing.

Within your business communications, you can often forget that your audience may have also mentally pressed skip before they reach the important bit of your message because the important bit of the message is somehow buried in the epic volume of words you are delivering. This topic is not limited to written communications, but about your need to effectively communicate all of your messages.

The truth is communication is less about what you say and more about why you say it, how you say it and when you say it. Even more importantly it is about what the recipient hears.

The first part of this process is to help you understand what good communication looks and feels like. Such as:

- Communicating why the recipient of your communication will be better off.
- What do you need the recipient to do as their next step?
- The right level of detail to supply in your communications.
- The preferred communication method for the recipient.
- The question of timing.

The second part of this process is to actively review the communication that occurs within your business starting with anything you create yourself. Then proceed to identify where could help your team improve on their communication and create a strategy to train and support them as they learn to become better communicators.

This book with its simplistic 'Why' and 'Method' format is deliberately designed to make consumption easy. Once you read this page about WHY you may want to put effort into creating an effective communication strategy it becomes easier for you to take the next step and read the following pages to work on the METHOD of creating a process.

Method

For years I have worked on crafting the most amazing and complete communications. Everything anyone could want to know would go into my messages. They were verbose. The better I got at writing, the longer they became and the less efficient they were in driving an outcome. Once I learned why that was happening, my communications returned to being short.

This chapter refers to all internal and external communications, both written in letters and emails and verbal scripts should you be sharing your communication over the phone or in person.

Part One – What makes great communication?

There are potentially just three parts to any communication.

1. What do you need them to know?
2. What do you need them to do next?
3. Why are they better off for reading it?

Most often people, including the old version of me, would start at step one writing pages and pages of content, giving little thought to the reader's ability to comprehend what I have to say. The call to action of a next step would be lost somewhere within the content or attached at the end. Finally, the subject would be factual, but bland.

The advice here is that you need to turn this the other way up.

1. Why are they better off for reading it?
2. What do you need them to do next?
3. What do you need them to know?

So, let's work through an example of internal communication. Think first about what's in it for the reader. In this case, let's presume you are setting up an offsite dinner for your team and you want to make sure everyone has been given the chance to give then opinion.

Subject: Have you say. Where do you want to go for the team dinner?

So, then we move to what we need them to do next and by when. This goes very soon after the salutation.

Please come back to me by email by the latest of Thursday 12th May to let me know which restaurant from the list below is your preference and any special dietary requirements. We will go with the majority vote.

Finally, we get to the body of the communication. Because we are writing this last, we already know what needs to go in. A list of restaurant choices.

The English Steakhouse
Chicken & Ribs
Vegan Surprise

If your communication has lots of content that you need to add, consider creating appendixes rather than having it all in the body area. For example, if you wanted to include the menus for these three restaurants add them as attachments to the email or on separate pages of paper. This is better than extending the email.

The finished email should look something like this. Short. To the point. No ambiguity as to why the recipient will be better off or what you need them to do next, how you want them to do it and by when.

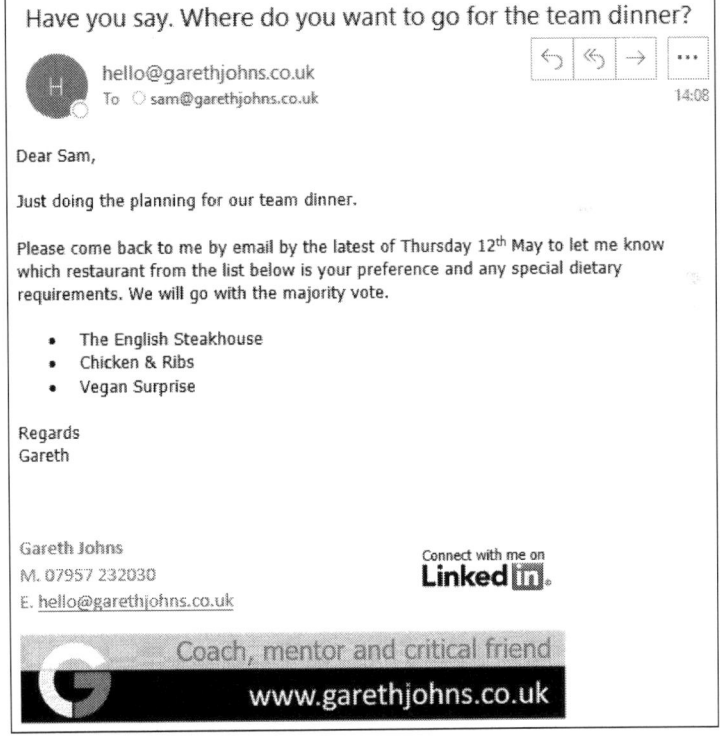

The last two sections of part one are your choice of communication method and the timing of what you send. This is going to sound blunt, but YOUR communications should be about THEM. Too often the authors of long missives are thinking about what they want to say, rather than what they want someone to hear.

With that out of the way, the next thing is a discussion about how you will communicate your message. If the audience for your message isn't 'email friendly', don't send emails. Pick up the phone or send them a Facebook message. So, start by thinking about how your audience would like to receive your communications.

Next, when would your audience want to receive your message. Again, I have been guilty of this. The best time for me to send a message tends to be at the end of the week and typically at the end of the day. So, let's say 4 pm on a Friday. My time has become my own and I can finally finish my task to send out some messages. But is that the right time for my recipients? If they are trying to clear their inbox to go home, would my choice to add to that pressure, just so it's off my jobs list, bring me the best level of response?

Part Two – How do you ensure your companies communications are great?

Now you have polished your output, you need to cascade this down through your team. If you have been verbose and unclear in your communications don't be surprised if your leadership team have followed in your footsteps and create similar messages.

As part of your leadership development, explain how you have amended your messages to your leadership team and review with them their messages. Ask them to point out how they could make the messages clearer and more succinct whilst providing more obvious details of why the recipient would be better off for it and what you need them to do next.

It is great news that communication is a learned behaviour. As such, although quite possibly your leadership team have some bad habits they can be retrained. It may take more than one run through but will be worth the effort.

Test all messages against these five points:

1. Why are they better off for reading it?
2. What do you need them to do next?
3. What do you need them to know?
4. What medium is best for them to receive this message?
5. When would be the best time to receive it?

Review the emails and letters you have sent out in the last few months and when you have sent them. Consider if you could have made clearer the next steps and why the reader would be better off? Consider if the timing of your messages were to suit you, or the recipient? Cascade this learning down into your leadership team.

Finally, as a footnote to this chapter and as I mentioned in the previous chapter, good communication contributes to your team's mental wellbeing too. Let me share a quick story about a toxic environment.

My mother was a schoolteacher and one of her frustrations was communication. She could learn what was planned for the school from the parents before she heard from the leadership. When this was investigated it transpired that the headmistress would have shared everything with the school secretary, who in turn shared what they knew with the playground gate supervisors, who would share their knowledge with parents as they came to collect or drop off their children.

Now of course, in this scenario every one needs to have the information that has been passed in due course. The issue is that it is being treated as power, or perhaps just gossip. The impact of information not arriving in a controlled way causes unnecessary stress which will detract from your work to improve the wellbeing of your team.

Ensure that company-wide messages are available to the whole team at the same time, even if not everyone in the team has had the chance to read the message. At least it was in their inbox or postal pigeonhole ready for them.

Company-Wide - Risk

The Why?

I find risk an interesting topic, but one that typically doesn't get much boardroom time. That is until you need to talk about the loss suffered because you didn't consider the risks you were exposed to.

This chapter is about helping you to identify and then think about them to mitigate those risks pre-emptively.

I am writing this book during the 2020 Covid-19 pandemic, so I guess we need to consider that as a risk too.

You may look at functional areas such as sales, delivery and finance as you consider your risks. When you are thinking about risks, don't only think about what you do today as a risk, but think of what you don't, but should or could be doing.

Although not an exhaustive list, here are few more headlines for you to consider.

- Company-Wide
- Reputation
- Competitors
- Becoming irrelevant
- Main office unavailable
- Dependency on a couple of customers
- Giving incorrect professional advice
- Financial exposure from aged debtors
- Suppliers
- Reducing credit terms
- Single source limitations
- Failure of a supplier
- Finance
- Cash flow and over trading
- People
- Team talent
- Widespread staff sickness

Method

There are essentially two attitudes that you can take to business risk. The most popular choice is to push any known risks to the back of your mind and pretend they don't exist. To put your head in the sand and hope that the problems just drift past you.

It's important to understand that the reason I believe that all businesses should have a plan to deal with risk is not just to avoid the consequences of that risk. There is a much more positive reason.

When I first started in business, I created a SWOT analysis and it was an eye-opening experience. This acronym stands for Strengths, Weaknesses, Opportunities & Threats.

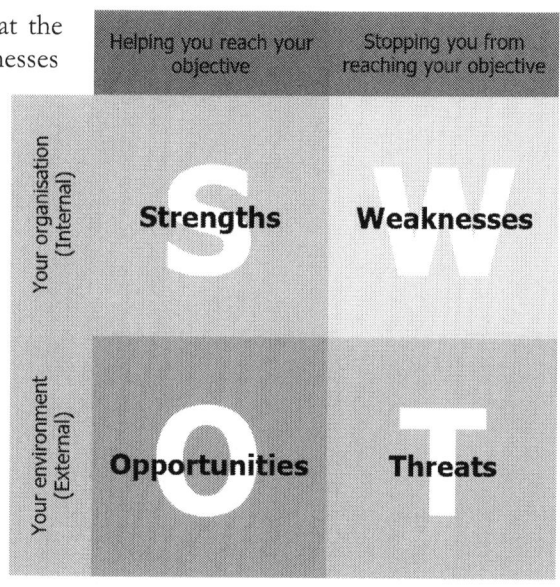

Although today it seems a little old-school, this is still one of the most valuable strategic tools if you understand how it can serve you best.

Step One

Pull your leadership team together at one of your strategic meetings to create four lists. To get the best out of this process you need to ensure you have trust in the room. If a system or process is weak or causing a threat to your business and the team don't feel that they can call it out, you also won't stand a chance of fixing it. If preferred you could use a business coach to help with this exercise.

Work through each of the lists in turn considering each of the operational areas of the business. How are you strong or weak in sales, delivery or finance etc. You must keep in mind your company vision as it only becomes a weakness or threat if it's going to stop you from delivering against your vision. Expect this process to take as much as a day to complete when you first work through this, albeit probably better handled as a couple of half-day sessions to keep energy levels high.

For this book, I have created some examples of what you may learn during your team meetings and created the following table. From this, you can consider what this means to you and your next steps.

Internal		External	
Strengths	Weaknesses	Opportunities	Threats
Product range	Lacking trained staff	Customer demand	No Google reviews
Employee loyalty	Office too small	Cross-selling opportunity	Limited buying power
Good with process	Lack of ideation	Wide available market	Quality issues

Step Two

You need to create a plan to resolve each of the weaknesses and threats you have identified.

Now it is possible that some things you just can't fix or perhaps can't fix right now. That's not a problem, just get some notes down regarding what you have considered at this point.

The ones you can resolve will ultimately become goals for members of your team. Remember, these will qualify as goals only because they are related to you delivering against your business vision.

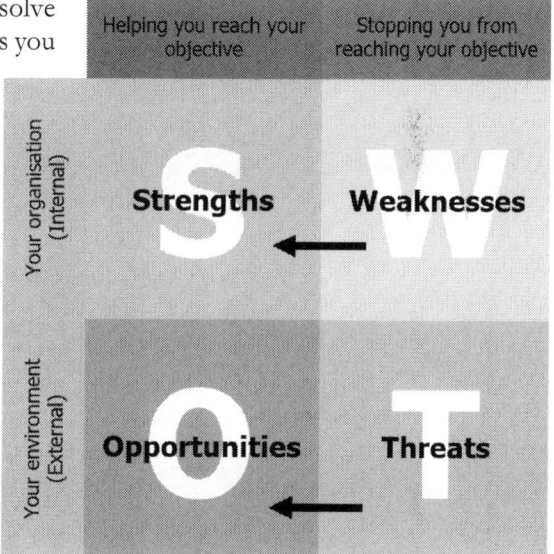

The purpose of this stage is therefore to turn weaknesses into strengths and threats into opportunities.

This is what it looks like based on our example data.

Internal	
Weaknesses	**Activity to become a Strength**
Lacking trained staff →	All staff certified to vendor excellence status.
Office too small →	Moved to a serviced office for scalable growth.
Lack of ideation →	Regular check-ins with the team to create new ideas.

External	
Threats	**Activity to become an Opportunities**
No Google reviews →	Create a Process to encourage all customers to create reviews.
Limited buying power →	Joined buying group allowing better pricing on current purchases.
Quality issues →	Process in place to continually review and improve quality.

Step Three

Weaknesses and threats often cause you embarrassment so you will do your best to keep them quiet and hidden from view. Strengths and opportunities, however, are the things you can shout about, but often you don't do enough of that either.

This step of the process is to consider everything on your strengths and opportunities as something that will help you achieve. Something you can leverage. Give some thought to each of your strengths and opportunities and what they mean to you and your business.

Internal	
Strengths	**Which means …**
Product range →	Great selection allowing a great fit for customer needs.
Employee loyalty →	Friends of existing staff are often suggested recruits.
Good with process →	It's worth adding more processes as they will be followed.
Trained staff →	Recruiting new staff into a great learning environment.
Scalable office →	Proven growth and continuing growth plan.
Ideation process →	The business continues to evolve and improve.

External	
Opportunities	**Which means …**
Customer demand →	The company has no excuse but to grow.
Cross-selling opportunity →	Opportunities to sell other products to existing customers.
Wide available market →	Opportunity to sell outside of the current geography.
Google review process →	Social proof of your provision available to new prospects.
Buying group member →	Opportunity to run as a profitable business.
Quality improvement process →	Now able to lead with quality rather than price.

Since starting this process, you have trained your staff, moved office and become a better place for your employees to call their place of work making recruitment and retention of new employees easier.

You have also evidenced how great your service is via collecting Google reviews, improved your buying prices and the quality of your offering. Your new marketing messages will be around quality products concerning the many customers who have said nice things about you. With your new buying price, you know you are more profitable too.

Step Four

As with all the advice in this book, you need to create a repeatable process. Within my business life, I would review my SWOT list annually as I update my business planning process. I would discover that some of the things I couldn't previously fix due to business scale, I could then perhaps make more progress. And as nothing is ever complete, I would discover new things for all four lists that I couldn't have predicted the year before.

Work with your team and create your SWOT analysis, complete with a list of things you can do to turn your weaknesses and threats into strengths and opportunities.

Finally, consider whether you are doing enough to maximise your strengths and opportunities.

Company-Wide - Community

The Why?

I guess firstly, I need to explain what we mean by community. Broadly this is everything outside of your business operation. For this chapter let us consider that to be under the three headlines of the business community, education and charity.

As to why this is important enough to warrant a chapter in this book, what I have learned is without a strategy for your community engagement, you will likely get caught up in things you shouldn't or do nothing at all, thus missing out on the potential benefits.

I am sure you are often approached requesting sponsorship or charitable donations. Having a community engagement strategy will help you understand which requests you should support and which you should decline giving an excuse of your budget already being committed elsewhere. Of course, this is coupled with you creating a budget for such philanthropic investments.

Documenting your community plan will allow you to think about how you can be generous with your money and time, whilst creating the best outcome for your business.

Don't worry if you think this sounds tasteless or even slightly narcissistic. True altruism doesn't even exist. If you enjoy helping others and most people do, you are helping others for your enjoyment.

The continued success of your business will only further enable you to be generous in the support of your communities.

Method

In the employment wellbeing chapter, I wrote about 'Community engagement opportunities' for individual employees, but this topic deserves its chapter. This is about corporate 'giving back', as people like to call it.

Controversially, Ricardo Semler said, "If you are giving back, you took too much.". This doesn't fit the capitalist dream but does encourage a win/win attitude throughout your life. Basically, you don't need to wait until you are done to help others, but you can and probably should do it throughout your time in business.

Here is the news. Unless you are successful in business, you won't be able to help your wider community. The next step here is to document a community plan, so you don't even need to feel bad about picking and choosing which projects you decide to support. Simply, the ones you support will be the ones that have a connection to driving your success. The ones that are aligned to your purpose, vision and mission.

There are three main areas to cover here:

Business Community

To become a person of influence in your business community, start by helping others. As such, if you are a member of a networking group, ask yourself what more you can do to help the group achieve. Can you teach the members something that will help their businesses to achieve?

Review any business groups you are a member of today. The two questions need to be asked in parallel.

Are you investing enough into the group?
Is it giving you enough of a return for your investment?

If the answer is 'No' to question one then it's your time to step up and help your fellow group members to be successful.

However, if the answer is 'Yes' to question one and 'No' to question two, you need to find another networking group that will return you a value from your investment. This is of course a tough decision to make as it's just possible that these group members appreciate you even if it's not helping your business.

Education

Nobody denies that children are our future. Today, do you do enough to help the education system prepare tomorrow's young people for a world of work? Your local schools will very much welcome your support around careers presentations that inspire children and give them hope for a future that is looking forward to welcoming them.

Could you provide apprenticeship opportunities leading to full-time employment within your company?

Charity

When I say charity, I also include not for profit community groups like youth sports clubs. This is probably the biggest potential opportunity to waste money if you don't have a plan.

During my time in business, I received many requests for donations, raffle prizes and sponsorship. In the early days, we just gave what we could. We however learned that often a £100 prize would help them sell £25 of raffle tickets, so a £100 cash donation would be better for the charitable cause. As such if this were a charity that we wanted to support, it would be better to separate our gifting from their raffle activity. We can then award the £100, or even better a tangible 'thing' that the charity needed. Where the raffle prize would be lost in the noise, the gift and subsequent photo opportunity for social media are easily worth £100.

Sports team 'club strip' sponsorship can be great for the profile. My business sponsored a youth team in Dover, which meant that every weekend there were hundreds of parents being exposed to our business branding. The occasional social media post when they won or when the team's coach posted pictures of his wife washing the kit between matches.

The last story of good works for this chapter is our sponsorship of Broadstairs Folk Week which is a not-for-profit festival that has run for over 50 years.

I chose to sponsor them for 20 years and the new employee-owners of BCS have chosen to continue this support.

In return for our commitment to them, they provide banner advertising that is in front of the 12,000 per day capacity. In addition to this, we tend to be able to bring some of our clients and prospects along to a live music gig or two introducing a few more people to the rich world of folk music.

The taxation issues around sponsorship contra opportunities are not something I am going to cover in this book. In the first instance, I just want to make sure you take advantage of how you can benefit from the organisation you are sponsoring and what it can do in return to help your continued success. Be creative and proactive in asking. You may be surprised what magic you can make happen that will set you apart from the rest of your business community.

Consider if you would like to create a place in your wider community and write down who you are planning to work with and what you plan to do for them. When someone comes to you asking for your help, you can check it against the list you made. You can also then plan to actively contact people you can help. Would you like to have a chosen local charity for the year so you can direct your activity in a focussed way?

People - Leadership

The Why?

Leadership is both a big topic to do justice to in a book like this, but also a fundamental skill that mastering will open the doors to your future business and personal success. But what do we even mean by leadership?

Leadership is sometimes defined as the art of motivating a group of people to act towards achieving a common goal. In business, this is about helping colleagues to deliver against the strategic goals of the business.

As a leader, if your direct report is successful in their role, that is thanks to their hard work and dedication. If they somehow fail to be successful, the responsibility for that will fall directly on your shoulders. That may seem unfair, but it's just how it is.

The next question is how you can make it more likely that your team members will succeed. What can you do to make it safe for the people you lead to make decisions, especially when those decisions may look like risks to other people in your company?

The lack of a strategic plan for leadership development typically leaves companies without a structure for having a second-in-charge for growth and resilience too.

By the end of this chapter, you will:

- Understand why and how great leaders build next-generation leaders.
- Know how to create a 'Team No 1' mentality.
- Know how to define authority and safely allow autonomy.
- Understand the benefits of allowing acting up ahead of giving employees fancy new job titles or additional salary.
- Define success whilst understanding when good is good enough.

Method

It will sound almost too simplistic when I tell you that working on your leadership skills will become the single largest catalyst for your business improvement. Within a few pages, I will share some of the most important things for you to consider as you create your unique leadership processes.

Why do people keep talking about leadership?

When I was starting a business in the 1980s, there seemed to be more books about management than leadership. Ultimately, both are about achieving objectives but they are massively different in their outlook as per this summary.

	Management		Leadership
Style	Authority	→	Coach and motivator
Rules	Follows blindly	→	Innovates to improve outcomes
Focus	Systems	→	People
Control	Retained as power	→	Given away to others
View	Immediate needs	→	Long-range perspective
Ideas	Imitates	→	Originates
Trust	Creates suspicion	→	Inspires trust
Questions	How and when	→	What and why

The difference can be summarised that the manager will **do things right**, whilst the leader will **do the right thing**.

The best leaders understand their role is to remove boundaries, focussing on what is possible and inspiring and supporting innovation whilst ensuring alignment with the business's purpose and vision. Leadership is often about knowing when to get out of the way, empowering others to achieve greatness.

For this chapter and any examples, let's assume you are the managing director and you have sales, delivery and finance leaders. Let's also presume you have brought an employee council president to your leadership team to ensure you have the voice of your employees heard at the board level.

Next Generation Leaders

A question I am often asked is **'How many people can a manager manage?'** to which the answer is hundreds. However, if the question is **'How many people can a leader effectively lead?'** the answer is probably no more than ten.

For you to be able to care and connect authentically with the people you lead, you must have time for them. My recommendation is that anyone in a leadership role should devote at least half of their time to the people they are serving as a leader and in the development of their ability to lead.

Great leaders don't just create results, they also create next-generation leaders.

For many years in my business, if one of my leadership team were to go on holiday, sick or leave I would consider it part of my role to cover their absence. This proved to be both unnecessarily stressful for me and a barrier to business success, because whilst I was doing someone else's job, I wasn't doing my own.

The time your leaders invest in their teams will ensure that each of your leadership roles also has deputies or second-in-charge colleagues who can stand in. For this to happen you also need to ensure that your leadership team sees this to be empowering to them and the business, rather than fear for their job security because someone could take over their job role at a moment's notice.

Work with your leadership team to identify second-in-charge people who can be developed to cover holidays and sickness. Document the core skills required and the gaps that currently exist.

Team Number One Mentality

I wrote in an earlier chapter about organisational structures and introduced the concept of a team number one mentality. This was originally defined by Patrick Lencioni in his book 'The Advantage' and I think you will find it a game-changer if adopted in your business.

Your problems and challenges are always greater than those of others. You feel and care about them more personally and they become the focus of your efforts, sometimes at the expense of everything around you. This issue will be repeated throughout your organisation.

As individuals, your sales leader will be troubled by the new business target they need to achieve; your delivery leader will be consumed by the requirement to process all the current orders and your finance leader will be gravely concerned about the overdue debt from your largest client.

Often, I see leadership teams come together to report, but not to ask for help. I listen to a series of monologues with a sensation that nobody is listening and even worse, nothing will happen because of those reports being given.

The alternative is to work as a cohesive team and so this is a lesson about being better together. Everyone on the leadership team is effectively in two teams. Team Number One and their team as below. They have two perspectives to bring.

- Team Number One plus Owners
- Team Number One plus Sales Team
- Team Number One plus Delivery Team
- Team Number One plus Finance Team
- Team Number One plus Employees

Team Number One cares about the company purpose, vision and mission. As such, they will agree to goals together and hold each other accountable for the delivery.

This approach ensures that the whole of the business develops in alignment. There is no point in having the best sales processes if you can't deliver what is sold or can't provide the cash flow to enable those orders.

Talk to each of your leadership team in turn and find out what they know about the company's strategic goals and how their department influences the goals. Then ask them what help they need and what help they can provide to team number one to ensure the strategic goals are fully met.

Authority vs Autonomy

Although there is some leadership magic buried in authority and autonomy, I want you to understand how one influences the other. Let's start with a definition.

- **Authority** – The power to enforce rules or give orders.
- **Autonomy** – The freedom to govern, act or function independently.

Effective and timely decision making is key to business success. Not all decisions will be amazing, but some will be and it's those decisions that will set your business apart from your mediocre competitors.

It's not unusual to one day realise that most decisions are back on the desk of the business owner, but what is the reason for this? Mostly, it breaks down into these two causes.

- **No clarity of authority given** – Sometimes, we are just not very good at defining what decisions an employee can make. A lack of clarity here will often create a lack of decisions rather than the wrong decisions. From a job security perspective, an employee will always feel safer deferring a decision rather than making a bad decision.
- **Overridden autonomy** – Even with the authority to make decisions delegated to your employee, it's not unusual to find you still have too much influence over the decisions they should be making. You can only override an employee's decision so many times before they stop making decisions, knowing that you will have the final say anyway.

As you can now see, authority and autonomy very much go hand in hand. You need to first define a level of authority for your employee and then leave your employee autonomy to make great decisions up to that defined level of authority.

Authority is best handled as an unambiguous written statement.

In one of my previous job roles, my boss wrote me a list to print and pin to the wall above my desk, detailing exactly what I had responsibility for and almost more importantly what was outside of the scope of my job role. As I faced a decision, I referred to his list and knew if I could act or needed to seek further authority. He was a great boss, so I never felt like he was second-guessing my decisions. That's not the same as saying he didn't have any influence, but I never felt like the decisions were overridden.

The last point to cover on this topic is how much authority should you give over to your employees.

My answer is, as much as you have in your role, but not all at once. In fact, at the start, you would give hardly any authority at all. Maybe just the authority to decide when an employee wants a break during the day and how long for. When an employee proves to themselves and you that they can cope with this, increase the amount of authority they have.

Mistakes will still be made but because it is within the boundaries of the authority the employee has earned the right to have, typically they can be accepted as learning experiences rather than catastrophes.

Your holistic one-to-one meetings each week are a great place to discuss this to keep the topic dynamic. Ask them to write down what they believe they have authority for today. Ask them how far they can go before they need to defer any decisions to you. You may be surprised or even frustrated about what you learn, but at least you can then start to act to safely empower them.

The benefits of encouraging acting up

When a vacancy appears for someone to join your leadership team you can choose to recruit someone new from outside your company or look to promote from within your existing team.

Two common mistakes with filling vacancies:

- **Internal promotion of existing unsuitable people** - I have often seen it tricky to fill leadership jobs offered to every member in the team in turn, in the hope that one of them will be able to do the job. This kind of recruitment is dangerous as often there is no route back to the job they could do well and enjoyed doing. Typically, the only way forward for the 'accidentally promoted' member of staff is to leave.

- **External recruitment of new unsuitable people** – Whether you place the advert and sift through the CVs yourself or engage a recruitment agent to help with this process, this is a big commitment in time and money. But it is often seen as the quickest and easiest way to achieve the desired outcome. The specification document you have crafted lists all the characteristics you desire and all you need is someone who claims to tick the boxes and they are in! For me, this recalls the scene in Mary Poppins when the children write the job scope when recruiting a new nanny. Your expectations are high and the recruit is typically given 3-6 months to deliver before you fall out of love, give up on them and start all over again.

As you will have noticed, what these two have in common is that on the face of it, they are both unsuitable people to work in these roles at your company. But what if it's not the people at all, but the job you are trying to fill that is the problem?

This was described by a mentor of mine as a soil and plant issue. The story is that:

A man went to a garden centre to buy the perfect rose bush, returned home and planted it in his garden, but within a week it had died. He repeated this process a few times, trying different garden centres to get better rose bushes but each time they didn't make it past a week.

It transpired that the soil was so acidic, no rose bush would ever survive. He adjusted the soil to create the right environment and purchased just one more rose bush that thrived. Yes, he needed to retest the soil periodically and make further adjustments to ensure it's still a healthy place for his roses, but his future is blooming.

The question therefore is, what if the people you recruit for these roles and subsequently let go are not unsuitable, but it's the job you are asking them to take that's not suitable for them.

If you have recruited more than one person for a role that has not worked out, use it as a warning that you should look closely at the job role. Specifically, investigate the clarity that exists for the employee. Do they understand what's expected of them and what resources they have available to them to deliver in their role?

If you are looking to fill a vacancy internally, there are many advantages of providing a trial period to allow a team member the opportunity to show they can deliver in the role. Don't be frightened to even make this a month or more. If the candidate will only step up for this trial on the condition they are paid to step up, I wager they are not the right person for the role.

At the point you make the promotion permanent, complete with a job title and revised pay, you will have removed most of your risks.

It will be worth investing a moment or two to review anyone who has left your company in the last 12 months and consider honestly what clarity the employee had regarding your expectations of them in the job role.

Definition of Success

Leading on from the topic of authority and autonomy is the challenges that arise when there is a lack of clarity about your expected success. As in, how do you know when you have achieved what you set out to accomplish?

More to the point, how would your employees know if they are doing their job well?

So that's two problems.

1. You don't have a clear view of success and what you do have, is only in your head with nothing written down.
2. Your employees have their view of success, but of course, that is also only in their head and not written down.

Without this success defined and shared, it is not unusual to find that your staff deliver something that to you looks like they don't understand what should be delivered. Over the next few pages, let's consider customer service as an example of where this mismatch occurs.

Picture a target with the bullseye being customer service perfection. You know clearly what you want your business to achieve and the level of quality and service you want to deliver to your customers.

In your head, nothing is simpler. If you and your employees just do the 'right thing' each time everyone will be happy and the business successful.

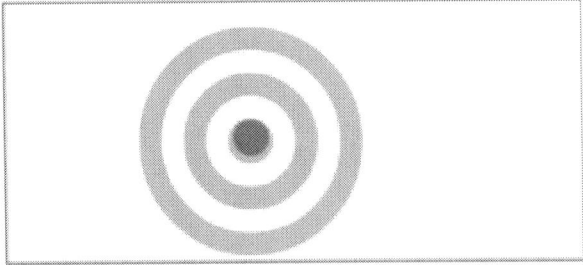

You believe that you have described it well and trained your people yet they don't seem to 'get it'. They deliver your service and come in at 80% of your expectation. Sadly, you can't even tell which 20% they are going to neglect to deliver on, so you end up double-checking the work completed by most of your team, ultimately destroying their commitment to you and your business.

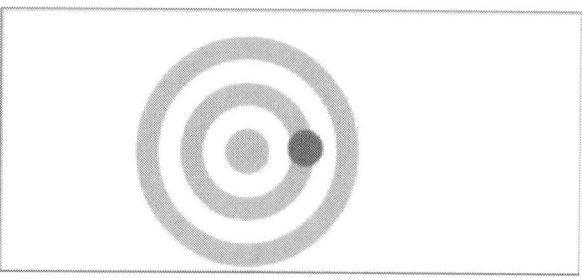

But here is the problem. Your employees don't have your eyes. However well you think you have explained your view of the bullseye, they will be seeing it through their eyes. Often when they hit 80% of your expectation, they are hitting 100% of their understanding of the target. Two targets are being used, whether you like it or not. You just presume the employee is somehow at fault.

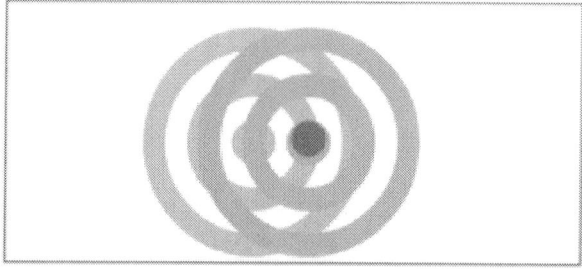

From my experience, it is not your target or your employee's target that matters, but the customers target. The customers view of the world. Does what you deliver meet or even exceed your client's expectations? If it does, how about defining that bigger bullseye and getting everyone in the company to get behind that instead?

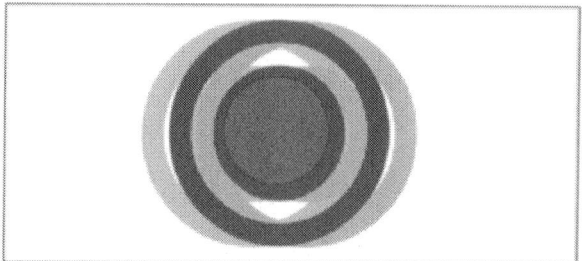

Perfection is pretty much impossible to achieve and you will die trying. Too many stress-related ulcers could have been avoided if instead of focussing on perfection we focused merely on excellence.

With all of that in mind, here are the next three steps you could take to help you accept that 80% of your target may be good enough for your customers.

- **Define Success** – What does excellence (not perfection) look like. Write it down. Don't approach this task in a vacuum but work with your team and don't be frightened to work with your favourite customers too. Make sure you listen more than you talk.

- **Review** – Have a process to review your delivery against your shared company definition of excellence. This is not something you should do every day, but something you come back to at a regular interval. You are not looking for reasons to beat your people up, but for opportunities to improve. Again, work with your team. Form a 'Quality Group' with members from across your business whose purpose will be to look for ways to impact the future.

- **Look for Bright Spots** – Identify the members of your team that deliver against the company definition of success. Use those as buddies for any new team members so they learn what your company's definition of customer excellence looks like.

Think about the things you do in your business because you don't believe others will do it well enough. Or the things you allow people to do but then double-check their workmanship.

What are the things that keep you awake at night or that your mind drifts to when on holiday when you should be focusing on that poolside mojito?

People – Effective Meetings

The Why?

Even the thought of thinking about meetings may put you off reading this page, but don't give up too easily. Effective meetings drive business success.

You can probably think of some meetings you have attended that have made a difference to you, your business and your future success. Sadly, there are fewer of those great meetings than the ones you leave muttering under your breath "well, that's two hours of my life I will never get back!".

When you drill into the difference between the two types of meeting you will find the successful one had focus. Clear objectives. The theory covered in this chapter is useful whether you are arranging a one-off crisis meeting or a regular pulse meeting.

All successful meetings will have considered the following five aspects.

- Purpose
- Frequency
- Structure
- Investment
- Outcomes

If you go out on the weekend to have a good time, you will have a good time. If you go into a meeting with a plan to sabotage the outcomes of the meeting with your lack of energy, or worse negativity, then you probably will! Effective meetings are impacted by the desire of all participants to have the best meeting.

Method

Before giving my business meetings focus, they were rambling, irregular, without structure, disrespectful of time, cancelled on a whim and often didn't drive change. The first meetings that I fixed in my business using this format were the leadership team's weekly meetings. Following success at this level, it became logical for the leaders to take what they learned and update how their teams meet too.

There are five aspects to consider when planning any meetings and it's worth working through these in turn whilst thinking about one of your regular team meetings.

1. Purpose

Meetings without a clear purpose tend to fail people's expectation. The clarity for every one of why the meeting has been scheduled is critical. Try to summarise the purpose of the meeting in a sentence.

Perhaps, "To keep the leadership team on track towards their quarterly goals and ensure they have whatever support they need." or "To work through any operational issues on project delivery".

My point here is the clearer you are about the purpose of the meeting the more likely it will deliver for all participants and less likely it will get derailed by the addition of topics that are not aligned to the purpose.

2. Frequency

The pulse of your meetings will in many cases drive the activity of the participants, so getting this right is an important factor in driving effectiveness. Too frequent and there is no time to complete the agreed actions and too infrequent and there is a chance that participants could have forgotten what they agreed to.

I remember when we first created a regular weekly pulse for our leadership team meeting and the pushback that I initially had. One of the meeting participants said in a frustrated tone,

> *"If I didn't have to attend all of these stupid meetings, I would be able to get some of my work done!"*

Following a few months of running these meetings successfully, that same person came to me and said,

> *"Gareth, these regular meetings are driving positive changes within the business."*

My point here is, when you create your meeting pulse, do it with confidence. Expect some resistance but don't give in quickly. If the meetings fail to deliver, it is unlikely to be the frequency that is the cause, but a failure to deliver against one or more of the other objectives.

3. Structure

Like a good story, meetings need a beginning, middle and end. The agenda should be standardised to ensure everyone understands the rhythm. They will also be time-bound ensuring the meeting respects the time it has been allocated.

Beginning - Part One

Open the meeting with something that gets everyone to contribute. This could be as simple as 'What's the best thing you have achieved this week' or 'What is your current mood and why'. If your meetings to date have only been an opportunity for you to tell your team what you want to say, this participative style may take a little while to become natural and may be uncomfortable for some of your team at first, but it's worth the effort.

There are many reasons for starting the meeting with an activity like this which include waking everyone up, raising the energy levels and ensuring they know this meeting will require their continued active participation.

Beginning - Part Two

For pulse meetings, it's essential you only talk about the things that need the attention of the participants of the meeting. As such, the second part of the beginning section of the meeting is to ascertain what you need to talk about. This should be a quick-fire section of headlines. Are sales on target? Are everyone's goals on track? Any customer or employee matters that need attention? If an issue needs some attention, add it to your issues list.

Middle

The list of what you could talk about in today's meeting will include everything you knew about before you started the meeting, plus anything that came out of your quick-fire agenda section. You now have a finite list of topics that need discussing but also a finite amount of time to talk about them.

In some cases, you won't have enough time to discuss all the topics on the list so the next thing to do is agree on which are the most important or business-impacting issues and discuss those first. Importantly, don't share the available time across all topics as that will result in none of the topics getting the time they need to be fully resolved.

Whatever less important topics you have left at the end of your allotted meeting time will be rolled over to the next meeting where you may have more time available to resolve them. From experience, often some of the less important topics 'resolve themselves' by the time you get to the next meeting.

End

Always allow enough time before the close of the meeting for two final activities starting with asking your notetaker to recap what has been agreed by all participants of the meeting.

Following the recap, ask all participants to give their score of the meeting perhaps out of ten. Of course, this is subjective. The attitude they brought along at the start of the meeting may impact their opinion of the meeting score. What is important in this section is to also ask what they feel could be improved to make the next occurrence a top-scoring meeting. Use this feedback to improve your meetings.

4. Investment

Having previously worked for a company where I felt that my input was not valued, but my attendance at the meetings was mandatory, I realised that there are different types of meetings. There are some meetings where you are encouraged to work together to solve problems and others where you round up your employees to tell them what you need them to know.

For the type of meetings that solve problems, ensure that the people on the meeting invite list all need to be there. Everyone around the meeting room's opinion should hold value to the meeting. If they are not there to contribute to the betterment of your business don't have them there.

5. Outcomes

We started this section by ensuring you understood the purpose of your meeting and the final step is to ensure you have clarity of the outcomes from your meetings.

Each recorded outcome will typically have three very clear elements.

- **What** are the next steps?
- **Who** will be taking them?
- **When** will this happen or be completed?

Ambiguity at this stage will leave meeting participants with 'wriggle room' to not deliver against their outcomes. Avoid the possibility that at your next meeting you will hear comments such as "I didn't know I was meant to be doing that" or "I didn't know it needed to be completed by then".

I recommend that the task of notetaker for meetings is assigned in advance including an expectation of them capturing the **What, Who** and **When** for all outcomes. If you are chairing the meeting, don't also take on the role of notetaker as it's both exhausting and missing an opportunity to engage one of your quieter members of the team into an active meeting role. These meeting notes should be distributed promptly to all of the meeting participants.

Agenda

To help you bring this all together, an agenda for a 90-minute meeting may look something like this.

> 10:00 – Meeting Open. Check-In Questions.
> 10:10 – Quick Review – Performance Figures – Any issues?
> 10:15 – Quick Review – Customer & Employees – Any issues?
> 10:20 – Quick Review – Goals Update – Any issues?
> 10:25 – Discuss Issues and agree on next steps.
> 11:25 – Recap outcomes and score meeting.
> 11:30 – Meeting Close.

What you will notice is that you have 60-minutes kept clear for discussing issues. It's key to ensure that the Quick Review sections are kept quick and are not allowed to become a discussion. It's either on track or needs to be added to the issues list.

Most people thrive on having a routine and keeping to a standardised agenda that drives outcomes. This will be welcomed by your team.

People - Shining Stars

The Why?

The North Star, or Polaris, is the brightest in the constellation Ursa Minor. With this knowledge, you can use your angle relative to this star to work out your location on earth. For more than two thousand years it has been used to help with navigation.

Sometimes we assume that our staff know what's expected of them. Imagine if I had just said navigate by looking into the sky, without telling you which star to use as your guide. Well, that's what we frequently do in business.

This chapter is about creating your definition of the 'shining star' behaviours you expect from your team.

If every member exhibits this same list of positive traits how amazing could your business be. Well, that is your goal.

To help you understand why it is important you define your 'Shining Star' behaviour I would like to introduce you to the concept of the 'Know Why and Know How Matrix'. This is also sometimes called the Will and Skill analysis.

You can be reasonably sure that when someone joins your company it is because they wanted to. They were willing to take the job and as such, you can consider them to be high WILL. They know WHY they come to work.

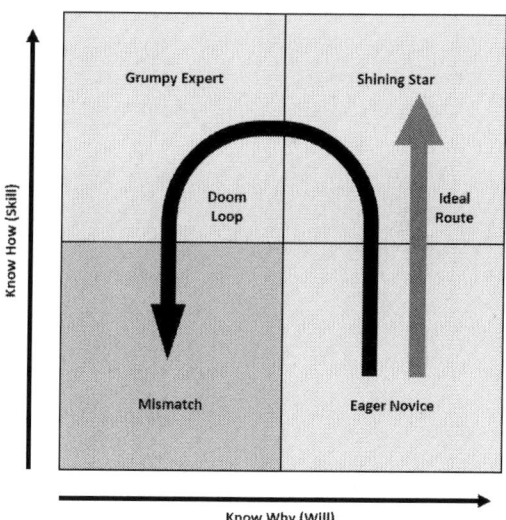

But they don't yet know what they are doing. Whether it's a new employee or an existing employee being moved into a new role it's the same challenge. They just won't yet know how to do their job as well as they will after they gain some more experience and knowledge. They are therefore likely to be low SKILL as they don't yet know HOW to do their job well. Your challenge in the development of your employees is to get them to high SKILL without losing their keen WILL to come to work.

Method

There are two parts to this exercise, starting with defining the behaviours of a model employee who is both high WILL, knowing WHY they come to work and who is high SKILL and knows HOW to do their job.

The second part is to see how you can work with your employees to mark their current behaviours and agree on the next steps on their journey with you to become one of your shining stars.

The impact of not having a definition of your 'Shining Star' and a way to help your team reach these heights will be that as your staff understand their job role better, they often also become less interested in working for you. Essentially high Skill but low Will. We call this the 'doom loop'.

I am sure you already have people in your team in mind as you read this. Some of these people are saveable, once they realise their behaviour is not helping them or the business. If you don't fix this quickly enough, their lack of interest in their job role will result in their learning interest waning too. Once they are low skill and low will, you are both better off going your separate ways.

One last thing of note here, in a business where you tolerate those with high skill, but low willingness leads to grumpy experts, the people who leave on their own accord are often the shining stars. They are the people who decide that they have two choices. To join the ranks of the grumpy experts or to leave and join a company where the employees are more motivated to help the business succeed.

You owe it to your shining stars to get your grumpy experts back on track or help them see that they would be happier and more fulfilled in a different role or even working for a different employer.

Step One – Definition

Define a clear view of what makes your business successful by way of ideal personal characteristics or behaviours.

You of course have your views, but don't produce this in a vacuum. This is probably a great exercise to invest 20 minutes of your team meeting to get the whole group of employees input. The question is "How do you expect a new colleague to behave?". You can share your examples and see what contributions your team offers. The advantage of 'workshopping' this list, is that it will be easier for the team to adopt as it will already feel like it is their work.

As you create your lists, don't labour too much about how you will measure adherence to each of these behaviours. Some will be easier than others to put numbers against. Try and create just one list that works company-wide rather than creating different lists for each job role as that will become very difficult to adopt.

When I produced mine as detailed below, I broke them into four subcategories which can help with discussions, especially during your holistic one-to-one employee meetings.

Customer Service

- Going the extra mile.
- Looking out for customer-impacting issues.
- Wanting to be better than our competitors.
- Great rapport with customers.

Team Skills

- Great social interaction.
- Acts as a mentor for co-workers.
- Assists peers with overcoming their shortcomings.
- Cascades knowledge to colleagues.
- Able to praise colleagues.
- Straight talking, no gossiping.
- Participates in the team structure.
- Honest and ethical in all dealings.

Knowledge Achievements

- Adaptable and effective learner of new skills.
- Taking an internal product 'Champion' role.
- Evidence of current qualifications.
- A study plan for the next qualification and the one after.
- An understanding of how qualifications benefit the company.

Commercially Aware

- Helping the customer engage about future work opportunities.
- Identifying customer requirements.
- Helping identify new revenue streams.
- Actively promoting the company brand.
- Protecting the company brand from being tarnished.
- Excellent time recording and managing workload.
- Disciplined, punctual and not frightened of hard work.

Step Two – Using the Tool

This is a great tool for all your leadership team to use periodically at their holistic one-to-one meetings. Use one meeting to talk about the behaviours, what they mean to the company and compare the employees understanding and your interpretation of them. Set homework to think about how they think they measure up against these behaviours.

The next week ask the employee to rate themselves against the behaviours for both Willingness (the why) and Skilfulness (the how) and draw an 'X' on the diagram.

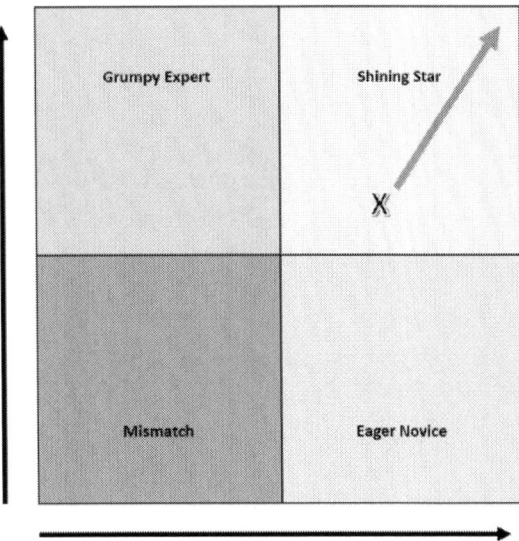

On the condition that an employee is sufficiently self-aware to not mark that they are in 100% alignment, where they put their 'X' is not as important as to understand they have a reason for where they are putting it.

In this example, the 'X' is at 70% willing and 60% skill. This score will allow you to lead a conversation to what can they do and what can you do to support them in their quest to become 100% skilled and 100% willing to achieve. Create some meaningful personal development goals based on this conversation.

Revisit this exercise about every quarter, so there is a greater chance for the employee to have made some progress on their behaviour goals.

People - Holistic One-to-Ones

The Why?

You should invest in the success of your people, so they are best able to invest in the success of your businesses. It is recommended that leaders have no more than about ten direct reports, so they can all have a good share of their leader's time every week.

It is not unusual for poor leaders to meet with their direct reports only in times of crisis, either for the individual or for the business. This gives a clear message that to get the leaders time they need to fail. The leader's role is not just to pick people up when they fall but to help them maintain their progress too. This one-on-one time should be weekly and therefore consistently scheduled every week.

Having this cadence means you are never more than a few days away from the opportunity to have a meaningful conversation. You can start to learn to defer your reasons to interrupt your employee with what you consider to be important and ask the same of them. They now have a scheduled time that is all theirs.

Your best people enjoy achieving their goals and enjoy the praise you should be giving. As such, there tends to be a spike of activity ahead of regular meetings, where tasks are updated. After the meeting, there is also normally some immediate activity.

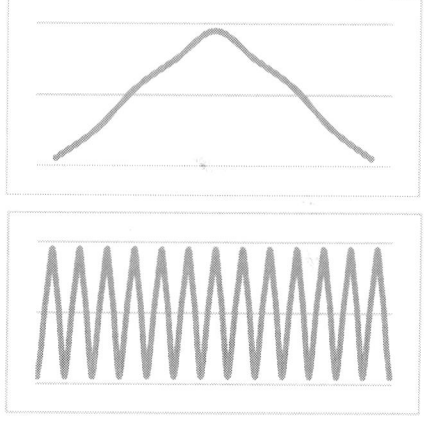

If you only meet quarterly, you only have one chance to make progress.

However, if you meet weekly, each quarter you have thirteen opportunities to help your team members to make real progress.

These meetings are not about pay reviews. I do wonder if leaders worry that their staff will always ask for things that the company can't provide or afford and for that reason, would rather not meet very often.

The truth is probably that your colleagues will deliver you more if they understand why it's needed and that's the purpose of these meetings.

Method

As I mentioned on the last page, the most important thing about weekly appraisals is to get on and do them, weekly. The second thing will be to give the meetings a consistent structure that allows the employee to feel comfortable and never ambushed.

There are three main topics you need to cover in an appraisal. Them, you and the company. There are theories that these should be given equal weighting, so in a 30-minute meeting, these will be 10 minutes each. However, if one of your team is having a personal crisis helping them solve that will be your number one priority and may mean you don't complete the agenda sometimes, which is okay. Always remember that you are investing in the whole of your colleague.

The location of this meeting is important. It needs to be somewhere private where you can both talk freely. Some colleagues will be happy to do these over a video call but for others, they will value time in a room with you. Most weeks you need to do what works best for them, rather than what is convenient for you.

Topic 1 – Them

How are they doing? This is their chance to speak freely to you. Your challenge will be to actively listen and consider everything they have to say. Take notes. Ensure you are ready to help if you can with their challenges, which may be to do with their work environment or even their home lives. It's their time. Their agenda.

Topic 2 – You

This is your chance to talk about their progress. Is their job performance allowing them to deliver 'their number'? Are they up to date with their skills development training targets? If you have issues noted from the previous week that you have decided would be best handled in private, this is your chance to discuss those matters.

Topic 3 - Company

This is the place where you want to talk about goals. Your direct reports goals should dovetail into your departmental or company goals. Their success is your success. Your role here is to help keep the goals on track. What can you do to support your colleague and what can they do to support you? As such, think short term and the week ahead. What can you achieve together in the next week?

A few additional considerations

- Advise your reports of the structure of these meetings so they can prepare for their opening 10 minutes. They may not have much to talk about for the first few meetings until they understand the rhythm, value and safety of these meetings.

- These meetings are not to talk about tactical, operational or client issues. If the issue could be discussed in the regular team meeting, it doesn't feature in the weekly one-on-one meetings.

- The meeting should take 30 minutes but always book them allowing an hour so you can overrun if you need to and have time to type up your notes and prepare for the next one. Investing an hour per week in each of your team is an investment well made.

- Don't be surprised or put off if your direct reports initially think this is a waste of their time or that it's a fad thing from you. Stick to the process and schedule, they will change their view and embrace your investment.

- And finally, another reminder that this is not a pay review meeting. Arrange that as a very separate meeting to this cadence.

People - Pay Structure

The Why?

The popular and easily asked question 'How much should I pay my member of staff?' has no simple or easy single answer, but that's what I am going to cover in this chapter.

By the time you are reading this book, you probably have employed some staff and if you are like most businesses, the salaries you awarded have no science behind them. You wanted a person to join you and they needed a certain figure to move. Perhaps you were worried that someone would leave you, so you paid more to keep them. Someone worked well last year, so you increased their pay this year in the blind hope that they will continue to work as well in future years.

Hopefully, by now you can see that the one weak element in this payroll negotiation is you. Having a documented plan will avoid future reactive responses to pay increase requests.

Thinking about creating a pay structure gives you chance to think about all the elements that impact payroll both this year and over time.

Peter Drucker is quoted as saying that "What you measure, gets managed." but I want to add my thought to that and say that "You deserve what you reward!". Of course, rewards include much more than just payroll, such as perks, praise, status and plain old job satisfaction.

The clue to knowing when you get your pay structure right is when your team consider it to be both fair and equitable. By this, I mean being impartial and treating people equally without favouritism. Having a robust and transparent pay structure will also help you avoid future pay discrimination claims.

You will need to avoid the type of pay structure that results in an employee being rewarded for actions that are not driving the company's success.

A good pay structure will also protect the business through more fallow times. As in, if a percentage of everyone's salary comes from the current success of the business in a downturn, the whole team will share some of the burdens of the slump.

Method

To start this section, I would like to share an example of when I got a pay structure spectacularly wrong.

Many years ago, I put together a scheme that gave employees pay rises for passing exams. These were qualifications we needed the staff to hold to retain industry competence. The outcome was that we had some staff who got on, didn't engage with the study options provided but worked hard and did their job to the best of their ability. This group earned badly. But those that invested their time in the training and gained the qualifications but didn't work very hard in their day job earned more.

You can only imagine the frustration that model created within the leadership and the workers? We got what we rewarded. We got what we deserved. A good pay scheme will incentivise the company's commercial success as well as the employee's engagement with any training programmes.

Something I learned late in my career is that there is a direct relationship between what you should pay your staff and how much you earn from them. I learned this from an inspiring American coach (he called it a W-2 multiplier) but for us in the UK, we can call it the P60 multiplier.

This can be used either to work out how much you can pay your staff or working the other way, how much you need to charge for your services. Of course, it will vary between industries, but for most 3x seems to work out about right.

If you know it costs you £25 per hour for your employee, as the fully loaded P60 cost, you can calculate that your charge rate needs to be £75 per hour. The £50 per hour between the two is used to run the other business costs including office, sales, transport and any admin costs. Finally, of course, you should also be left with some profit.

Working back the other way, if you have a charge out rate of £60 per hour, divide by 3 and you will learn you can afford to pay your employee £20 per hour. The question then becomes if £20 per hour is not enough, should you consider increasing your charge out rate?

Of course, you will also need to work this out across the year and the whole team. Let's consider a business with four staff whose services are charged out with revenue from their services in the year of £600,000. Divide by 3 = £200,000 you can afford to pay out in wages.

You now need to divide that by the four staff and this is where it gets interesting as that £200,000 doesn't need to be shared equally but it should be shared fairly. By this I mean, someone who works harder or more effectively may be due a greater share than the person who comes to work, does the minimum, leaves mayhem in their wake and mentally clocks off an hour before they finish work for the day.

If you paid each of the four fee earners £40,000 each, so £160,000 in total you have a remaining £40,000 available in a bonus pot.

The next question is what behaviour from your fee earners is aligned to your mission and will help your business achieve your vision. Take another look at the list you created in the 'Shining Stars' chapter in this book. Reward that behaviour as that's what you want more of. If you reward the right behaviours your overall fee out will go up and a third of that new total will leave you with even more in the bonus pot to share out.

From experience poor things to reward include total time recorded, total jobs completed. Better things to reward include bringing projects in on budget and customer satisfaction.

The biggest challenge to introducing a scheme such as this will be the people you already pay too much and are not aligned to the business goals. Typically, these are the 'grumpy experts' who need to be realigned or helped to leave your business. I have found that offering someone with a current wage of £45,000 the chance to take a new contract with a base wage drop to £40,000 with an opportunity to earn an extra £10,000 from their performance will either get them on board or they will leave. Either is in my opinion a positive outcome. And of course, all recruits will settle in to enjoy the new scheme and never know when performance was not rewarded.

I remember within my IT business we adopted an approach where we paid the engineers a fixed and standard base wage, with bonuses calculated on how many charged out hours were delivered without any remedial work required. This produced both an increase in work output and a quality of service, which in turn helped improve customer satisfaction.

The remote support desk area of my business had a relatively high turnover of employees. At one point I would write that off as being a symptom of 'Generation Z' or something that was out of my control, but it turns out I was wrong. It was mostly down to not providing a structure and a route map to the way forward.

The scheme we put in place for the remote support desk area was that these employees would at interview have the opportunity explained and their expectations managed. By joining us they would understand that their base wage would increase every six months for the first three years, but only if they also met their agreed training plan outcomes. By three years, the idea is that continuous development in their skills will have become a habit and the base wage would be about what you would need to pay a new starter with the same level of education. In addition to this base wage, they would of course also be able to receive additional bonuses based on job or team performance.

Then onto the admin team. Although you can't link these staff directly to their fee out, you can create a similar model whereby you reward the behaviours that drive your business success. Maybe innovation, process improvement or just committing to working hard in the support of the rest of the team.

One of the important things to consider as you put your new pay structure together is that you need to be able to communicate what is expected of every employee. What they need to do to gain business recognition and if applicable earn more.

Start this process by making a list of the behaviours that are aligned to your mission and would drive your business towards your company vision.

People - Profit Sharing

The Why?

This topic is not for the faint at heart, but remember fortune favours the brave.

Logically this follows defining a great 'Pay Structure' from the last chapter. If you consider base wages to be bread, personal job performance rewards to be butter, then this section about company profit is your favourite jam. Without jam, bread and butter is food but with jam it's lunch.

Firstly, let's get the question 'Why should I share MY profit with the staff?' out of the way which I believe splits into these main reasons.

- **Motivation**
- **Staff Assumptions**
- **Business Thinking**
- **Difference & Retention**
- **Scale**

If you are considering putting a profit-sharing scheme in place, there are four main questions you will then need to answer.

- **Percentage**
- **Inclusiveness**
- **Distribution**
- **Openness**

Work through this chapter and then consider if sharing some of your profit could bring you the staff behaviours that will result in you creating more profit than you do today.

Method

In tough times you expect your team to show resilience in the face of adversity. When business is lean, you will ask your team to forgo their pay rise or even take a pay cut so you can trade through to a better day.

We are not always as quick to share the good times with our team. Or at least not proportionate to the success of the company. When you have a good year financially, you may elect to buy the wine at the Christmas do, but that's not the same as paying off your employee's credit card debts. Rarely in a good year would you share just how good your year has been with your team for fear they will think as the business owners you are greedy.

Let's start this section by exploring the reasons you may wish to consider sharing some of your profit with your employees.

- **Motivation -** It has been well documented over time that profit incentives drive a feeling of ownership. Implemented well they cause an increase in productivity and employee satisfaction.

- **Staff Assumptions** - You can bet that your staff think that you earn more than you do from your business today.

- **Business Thinking** - As your team realise that their profit share is calculated on how profitable the business is, with encouragement, thinking changes across the whole staff group. Whether that's thinking about new products, improving processes or just not wasting paper towels in the staff toilets.

- **Difference & Retention** - Not all business owners will make this leap and as such, you can use this as a point of difference to attract the right talent. There will be people in your team who could be described as 'wantrepreneurs'. Attaching these people's needs to the profits of the business will provide them with the connectivity they need to thrive.

- **Scale** - This is more easily explained with numbers. Let's assume today you make £50,000 a year in profit and 100% goes to you as the owner of the business. If you gave away 25% of the profits and that drove the behaviours that pushed your profit up to £100,000. You would give £25,000 to the staff, but your share has just risen to £75,000. 75% of something big beats 100% of something smaller.

For my IT business, I chose to give away 20% of the net profit to the staff and it was shared equally amongst all the employees. The lowest-paid staff used the bonus to pay off their debts and the highest-paid staff would buy virtual reality goggles.

Of course, profit figures are a trailing statistic. As in, it's a number that is 'after the fact' so you may say that the employees can't influence it. As such, it is key that you can help the team understand the company monthly or quarterly budget and how they can directly impact it, rather than just report the profitability when it's too late to help the company achieve.

My experience highlights the four questions you need to answer.

- **Percentage** - How much of your profit are you willing to share with the team that created the profit? Whatever you choose to pay as part of a profit share forms part of the total pay package. Payments made like this also protects the business as if the business is having a poor time, the lack of profits will mean that the bonus is not earned.

- **Inclusiveness** - Will this scheme be for everyone in the team or just certain favoured members? I often find but am no longer amazed that business owners first thought is to introduce a profit share for the leadership team only. You could do this of course, but it won't deliver against the five reasons why you may want to share some of your profits.

- **Distribution** - Will this scheme be based on existing salary, so those that get paid well will also get higher amounts of the profit share? Again, I have seen both put into place with varying levels of success. If every job role in your organisation has a base wage plus an individual or small team performance pay element, then this final companywide profit share element can be handled in a much more open way. The more even your distribution, the more it will motivate and the easier it is to talk about.

- **Openness** - Are you ready to be open with your team about the success of your business? If you choose to include everyone and distribute the profit share evenly, you can talk openly about your current level of success and what is needed to achieve your targeted success. This may also mean you need to teach some fundamental accounting to your team and ensure that each member of the team knows what is within the scope of their job role to influence the profitability of the business.

When we put our profit share into place it was initially greeted with scepticism from both the employees and my business peers. Over time it started to bring the right behaviours that brought the right results. Nothing creates a more cohesive team than the feeling that we are all in it together for the bad and for the good times.

People - Recruitment

The Why?

This may prove to be a bigger topic than you would think from the title. To help you understand why you need to put more effort into planning your recruitment, here are some of the headlines we need to consider that will improve your chances of a successful and repeatable process.

- **Proactive** – Many businesses recruit in a hurry often due to a lack of foresight of the need for additional team members.

- **Applications** – This section could have almost been in the 'sales' section of this book. What do you do to sell the benefits of working at your company to drive the application process?

- **Salary** – As part of this chapter I want you to consider the impact of the phrase 'Pay based on experience' and consider an alternative approach.

- **Cloning** – The danger of thinking this is the best way to expand your team.

- **Interview** – Relaxed informal interviews have their place, but only as part of a structured process.

- **Onboarding** – A positive experience for your new employee needs planning and will create clarity of your expectations too.

For some readers, recruitment in the past has been a simple case of whether you use a recruitment agent or post an advert on a job board yourself. Over the next few pages, I will help you understand these six main considerations to ensure that as you create your processes, they will deliver you a consistent level of success.

Method

I have never been naïve enough to assume that it is possible to produce a 100% successful and repeatable recruitment process. What you can do however is tip the odds in your favour using a few simple steps.

Proactive

The first self-inflicted challenge is that lots of recruitment activities are reactive. By this I mean we perceive an immediate need for a new skill or an extra person. Because we didn't predict our needs, we tend to rush causing poor outcomes.

To avoid this, have a business plan that predicts your need for additional staff in alignment with your business growth. Recruit ahead of your needs to allow time for an effective onboarding and initial training process.

Of course, that plan won't work seamlessly when you need to replace someone that leaves you in an unplanned way, but at least at the point that happens, you will not already be on the back foot trying to manage a labour shortage. One leaver should become easier to deal with if your leadership team's processes have ensured you have a 'second in charge' for all key roles. When you get good at recruitment, ideally you will have your 'next hire' lined up in reserve, which will accelerate this process.

Applications

Even businesses that are great at selling their products and services are often not good at selling the benefits of working for them. Yes, there may be times when you need to be working with recruitment agencies, but you also need to be deliberately receptive to applications coming from recommendations and even encourage them.

There is also a lot you can do to shape the applications you review, starting with creating a job specification. I have seen this presented as a single page of requirements and expectations, but the best versions are more like a sales brochure. There is an example 9-page brochure as a PDF you can download from my website at www.garethjohns.co.uk/bbb

The job specification should include:
- Company – Your purpose and maybe your core values.
- Person Specification – Responsibilities and the type of person you seek.
- Details – Pay structure and training offered.

Salary

On a job advertisement, what does 'Pay based on experience' mean?

For the employer, it normally is an indication that you hope to get someone in the advertised post at the lowest possible rate that you can get away with.

For the potential employee, however, it means that they need to believe that you will value their experience to the point that you may pay enough for them to consider coming to work with you. As such, they need to apply just to find out more, potentially wasting your time and theirs.

The alternative is to offer pay within a scale and this is where I want to help you in this chapter. Let's say for argument that you would be willing to pay between £25,000 and £30,000 for your next hire, which is for a production supervisor within an electronics business.

By advertising the range, you will help people who need a £50,000 salary avoid applying just to learn more.

Long before the interviews, define what these two fantasy employees look like at either end of your scale. The bottom figure is your minimum viable employee for the role you advertised. If they don't even meet these criteria, without any further thought you know that you can't employ them. The top figure is the person who would help your business achieve success by their performance in the role.

Think of the skills that matter most for the position you are advertising.

	£25,000	£30,000
Education	A-Level	Degree Level
Production Experience	1-Year	5-Years
Soldering Iron experience	1-Year	3-Years
Management Qualifications	CMI Level 3	CMI Level 5

As you sift the CVs you can match up where you believe they fit from a pay salary point of view before you interview them.

The magic in this process is that when you offer someone a job at a rate between minimum viable at £25,000 and their worth, you will also know what the initial gap is between the offer and the top of the pay scale. This will form the basis of the career development path for the new employee, as you know that the company will be better off with the £30,000 employee.

Cloning

Naturally, your first hires tend to be people who are like you. This generally leads to an amplification of everything great about you but it doesn't scale well.

Once you have a few employees, this ceases to be the right way to recruit as it becomes an amplification of everything you are deficient in too.

By creating your organisational chart (guidance in the Company-Wide section of this book) complete with the role's key responsibilities, you will come to understand the skills and personality types you are looking to recruit. Focus on this and the recruits hired will complement your existing team.

Interview

There are two distinct parts to this section.

1. Interview Questions

Typically, questions are made up ad-hoc, based on what you can see on the application form or resume. The questions should be related to the job role you have in mind and even better if the questions will give you an insight into the applicants capacity to progress within your organisation.

Does this person have leadership potential? Could this person one day be the new Managing Director? Your core values will play a big part in the interview process. Prepare your questions ahead of the interview.

2. Interview Process

People behave differently depending on their environment and the best advice I was given some years ago is to interview in an environment matching where you expect them to work. If you are looking for someone to carry bricks on a building site, interviewing them dressed in suits across a board room table is probably not very relevant or a fair environment to judge them in.

There are also advantages of having your interviewee interact with several members of your leadership independently, so you can meet after to compare notes and decide if they make the shortlist of possible new hires.

Perhaps three lots of 20 minutes. A casual chat when they arrive, the formal interview (the right amount of formal for the role) and finally a tour of the office. Look for how they act and react to their potential colleagues. Are they interesting and interested in what is going on around them?

As part of your interview process, it is a great practice to invite the candidate back for a trial day to meet their colleagues. Importantly, you want the potential new team member to do their job tasks whilst being supervised by a colleague to ensure their actions do not cause any customer quality issues. Avoid the temptation to just show them what you do, as that won't help them or you get the value from this stage. The supervising colleague may need some coaching so they know what to look out for as they support this stage of the interview process.

Finally, round up all that great feedback, select your new team member, make the job offer in line with your pay structure and if accepted, take up employment references every time. Go back at least three jobs if there is a career history available. Mostly you are looking for responses that align with your business core values. Remember to ask for shirt sizes too, so you can get their workwear ordered.

Onboarding

Invest the time now to create a formal structure for onboarding new colleagues. This will set them up for success. Making it easier for them to succeed in their new role than to fail. There are five main things to think about here.

1. Itinerary

Chart the time from 09:00 when they start work on their first day to the end of their probationary period. This should hopefully include a chance to meet most colleagues over the first couple of weeks, understand the workings of the business, complete all mandatory probationary training, attend weekly one-to-one meetings and any team meetings.

If you remember back to your first day in a new year at school, you start by populating your school planner with your lesson and classroom details. Give at least that level of clarity.

2. Probation Expectations

Even with a structured itinerary, you should ensure your new employee understands what is expected of them. Assuming you have some idea of how will measure this employee's performance, introduce it early in the probation.

If their behaviour will influence their ability to perform, point out what those behaviours look like to the company. Too often behaviours and performance measurements are only talked about when it is felt that someone is not working as expected.

3. Team Resources

During the early weeks of an employee's probation period, they will need the support of colleagues to learn. This time needs to be booked in and how the time will be used planned. My advice is also to use colleagues who you consider to be the most aligned to your company core values to train your recruits.

If you can't afford the time to support the learning of your new starter, this may not be the right time for you to recruit. This again is one of the reasons why you should always plan your recruitment strategically ahead of having an immediate need.

4. Material Resources

If you need a desk or computer to be ordered for your new starter, don't leave ordering it until they turn up for work. You want the recruit to turn up ready for work, so you need to uphold your side of that work ethic and be ready.

One last thing about material resources. There is a real negative impact of giving your new starter the slowest computer in the office that crashes a couple of times a day and a 5-year-old mobile phone you found in the back of the drawer. You have spent thousands in recruitment costs to get to this point, don't scrimp on what is important to the success of the hire.

5. People Impact

The decision your new employee took to join your company was probably not made in isolation but included their significant other and maybe even their family. Their decision may have caused unknown family repercussions. What could you do to show you value the decision they have made? Perhaps a thank you card for their partner or a meal voucher for their family?

Sales - Lead Generation

The Why?

Using the methodologies of this book and the work you have undertaken to define your medium-term goals for growth in your business, you now have a very clear understanding of how much new business you need to hit your goals. A long time before we can celebrate or ring the sales bell, we need to create some new leads.

An effective lead generation system will produce a consistent and manageable flow of enquiries, whilst maintaining spending within your agreed budget. Sometimes this is called a marketing plan, but please ensure you don't think of marketing as advertising. What is important here is that your process also includes all the available lead generation pillars.

For your business sector, there may be others, but within this chapter, I would like to cover off the following topics and talk about why you need a plan to harness the power of each.

1. **Testimonials & Referrals**
2. **Website Content**
3. **Social Media**
4. **Authoritative Voice**
5. **Clever Marketing**
6. **Simple Marketing**
7. **Watering Holes**
8. **Sponsorship & Philanthropy**
9. **Events**

Over time, the chances are that your prospects will have been touched by more than one of your lead generation activities. As such, when they become a valuable lead it is often hard to determine the 'point of attribution'. Was it the advert they saw or the letter that landed on their desk that made them pick up the phone?

The caveat here is that all lead generation activity poorly executed will consume as much money as you are willing to throw at it. Measuring the effectiveness and engagement from all activities is therefore important.

Method

Before you can create a plan, you will need to set yourself a budget for lead generation. However, even ahead of that you must know what the Life-Time Value (LTV) of a new customer is likely to bring your business so you can then calculate the Customer Acquisition Cost (CAC).

- **Step One** - As an example, let's look at a window cleaning business. We will assume that it costs £30 per clean and they visit the customer every month, so they have an annual income of £360 (12 x £30).

- **Step Two** – Moving on from turnover (sales receipt value) they need to deduct the cost of sales. I don't know about window cleaning businesses, but let's assume for this example that it costs 45% of every sale to put a person in a van with the tools to do the job. Therefore, in nice round numbers, they will spend £160 on the 'cost of sale', which will leave them with £200 (55%) of gross margin. This will be used to pay the rest of the infrastructure, admin, accountancy and of course, new business lead generation costs.

- **Step Three** – Find out either from industry data or trading history how long a customer typically remains loyal. For our example let's presume a good window cleaner can keep a customer for 5 years, which means that over the life of the customer they will have collected as the LTV £1,000 (5x £200) in gross margin.

- **Step Four** - The next figure we need to calculate is the Customer Acquisition Cost (CAC). In simple terms add up all the new business sales and marketing activity costs and divide it by the number of new customers taken on over the same period. It is normally expected that you may need to spend 20% or more of your LTV to acquire a new customer. Let's assume 20% for this example, which means the window cleaner can afford to pay £200 to acquire a new customer.

Keeping it simple has been the aim of this book. The rest of the chapter will focus on how to spend the £200 budget that we now know we have available to attract one new customer to this window cleaning business. Don't forget that this budget is to cover both your internal labour and any augmented labour you need to recruit.

Businesses with low margins, non-repeating income and no real customer loyalty will have much less in their budget for customer acquisition but the principals are the same. Start with the numbers.

Marketing on the peak versus marketing in the trough!

During the **start-up** phase of a brand-new business, the founders typically have plenty of time and energy to focus on getting the first customers. At some point, the business gets **too busy** and whatever the founders were doing successfully to bring in new customers, they stop doing. After a while and a few customer losses, the realisation that new customers are not naturally or organically arriving creates a **panic mode** where new types of marketing are started in the hope of getting new work. Eventually, the business will stumble across something that works and get back into the **recovery** phase of their sales ambitions.

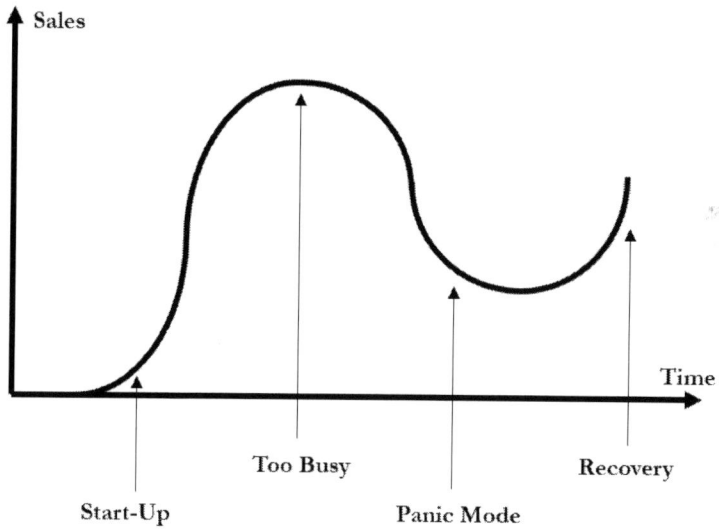

Marketing efforts that are started in a hurry as a knee-jerk reaction to a perceived critical need for new customers tend to be less strategic, cost more and have a lower level of success from a repeatable process point of view.

Of course, sometimes you will just get lucky and that's great, but if you would rather not bet the house on the hope of one spin of the roulette wheel, let's ignore hope as your new marketing strategy and focus on creating a plan.

Your new plan will be to invest in marketing consistently including when you think that you are 'too busy' to do any marketing. This will help you avoid the negative business and financial impact of the troughs.

On the first page of this chapter, I provided a list of 9 possible headline marketing pillars. Some you will have heard of and others may be new to you. Several are expensive to explore and others much more affordable.

1. Testimonials & Referrals

A referral is typically just that a customer will vouch for you and your business as a supplier. A testimonial on the other hand is a story about how you and your business identified a problem, solved it and delivered a positive outcome. How many testimonial stories do you have documented today?

If lots of your prospects are in the same sector, the chances are they will face the same challenges and therefore identify with the testimonials you have collected. Use the right story for the right prospect.

Having the task to harvest new testimonials each month will ensure you have plenty of current stories that you can use within your marketing and sales prospecting activity. Knowing you have this bank of ready-to-go testimonials, you can plan to use these in your sales process.

2. Website Content

Your website being current is more important than it has hundreds of pages. A single-page website of the information that a prospect is looking for will always win against a much more detailed, but hard-to-navigate out-of-date alternative. Your website should be about the problems you solve and not about you. It should also have very clear methods to connect with you and why the reader will be better off to do so.

If you have a blog or news section on your website, have a plan to get something meaningful and informative posted there at least monthly. Of course, it's also great to let the world know that you sponsored something or wore jumpers for charity, but those 'fluffy' articles should be extra rather than the only thing you post.

It varies between business sectors, but we know that by 2020 about half of all website viewing was via mobile devices. As such, you must ensure that any visitors from mobile devices get the same professional image of your business as from your desktop version.

Once you have a current website that converts visitors to prospects, it may be worth considering paying search engine providers such as Google to promote your website but consider this a way of amplifying your activity rather than fixing a broken system.

3. Social Media

There are many social media platforms. Many new ones are launched and die out each year. Different age groups seem to have their favourites and of course where businesses often will choose LinkedIn as their platform of choice, if you have a product you sell into the consumer space, Facebook and Twitter are probably your number one options today.

What does seem to be important about all the social media platforms is to dedicate time to listening rather than just speaking. You can learn a lot about your prospects from what they post. You will find out more about their pain, so your language can directly target this.

I am sure I won't be alone when I admit that I don't understand how to harvest some of the commercial benefits of the newer upstarts such as TikTok. What is important is finding out which platforms are favoured by your prospects and placing your time investment there, rather than thinking you can be a player on all platforms.

Finally, most of the platforms have paid-for options to promote your posts so they are seen by audiences wider than your contacts. Be careful here as if you have not segmented your list correctly to be just your avatar prospects, having an unclear message or a non-compelling call to action is a quick way to spend all your available budget gaining limited success.

4. Authoritative Voice

Do you have an opinion? Do others value your opinion and base their decisions on your advice?

Picture the conversation that starts with a friend asking you "I am looking at buying a new lawnmower. Should I buy an electric one or a petrol engine?". Would you say, "Not a clue and I don't care as I live in a flat"? Or would your research, experience and knowledge lead you to say something like "Electric mowers have improved in the last few years and it's worth considering a cordless model now for convenience, reduced weight and limited servicing requirements"? In this second response, the friend would leave more knowledge knowing their next step is to research cordless mowers.

What I am saying here is, if you have the knowledge and share it you will be viewed as having an authoritative voice.

It could be that right now, there are not many people asking you for your opinion but that is probably not because they wouldn't value your opinion, but more likely that they just don't know you exist.

Who does your local chamber of commerce, the federation of small business, trades guild, business networking groups or even newspapers turn to when they need an expert's opinion for something in which you are an expert?

When the next interesting change happens to your business sector, contact everyone who runs groups of potentially interested people that align with your avatar prospect and offer your services to either write an informative article for them or speak at one of their meetings. This is not a pitch for your services.

If you are not confident to speak see if you have anyone else within your business who would love the chance to develop these skills. As I have previously told all first-time speakers, the first time won't be as great as you hoped, but the second time you speak you will be better and more focused on the recipient of your efforts. Speaking is a learned skill.

5. Clever Marketing

The more you know about your prospects the more likely your messages will resonate with them. By this, I don't just mean what you say but also how you say it. For example, in the IT Sector for years they have wanted to call what they do 'Managed Service Provision' but it transpires that the prospects are just searching for 'IT Support' in their local area. Using the right words matter.

To help you here, interview your existing customers, especially your most recently acquired customer contacts. Find out what they value about the relationship. The speed or quality of service? Your strategic intent? The problem finder and solver nature of your relationship? You are looking to find the pain that engaging you took away in their language.

You can then take this newly discovered information and craft messages to put directly in front of businesses that are like the ones you interviewed. Likely, the pains of businesses in the same sector will also be similar. When they read those messages, they will more easily identify with your proposal and your call to action.

6. Simple Marketing

Although I have put this at number 6 in my list, it's probably one of the easier and most overlooked in the desire to get smart. If you are in a business-to-business environment, do you have a list of prospects companies you wish you could work with? What do you know about them? Do you have the right contact details for the influencers and decision-makers within each? Who are their current providers of what you could provide for them?

I have had amazing success with just sending some well-crafted letters or emails at the right time. Lumpy mail such as a letter with a chocolate bar to the right people can have a great impact if not overused. Knocking doors or picking up the phone is often seen as the dirty end of marketing, but sometimes they can still work well.

7. Watering Holes

Think about the business sectors you serve. Solicitors, Estate Agents, Construction, Manufacturing etc. Where can you go to directly meet with people in this sector? Where do these people currently 'hang out'? Where is the watering hole they attend to drink in the knowledge they require to learn and improve their businesses?

What conferences or exhibitions do they attend? Can you attend as footfall, take a stand to exhibit or even speak with your authoritative voice? Remember, all your messaging will be about the sector you are getting close to. It doesn't matter that you serve multiple avatars businesses, it matters that you understand this one fully.

8. Sponsorship & Philanthropy

There is the potential for a reciprocal value from sponsorship but sometimes often you must look for it or even be creative in the design of any sponsorship deal.

Getting your logo on the football shirt is great, but it's what happens next. Questions you should ask are who watches the team you plan to sponsor? And would your existing customers and prospects be interested in the success of this team?

Your town team may only be of interest to people in your town. If the people who attend the home game matches are typically not connected to your prospect customer, you are getting some name awareness but limited opportunity to convert these avid football fans into raving fans of your business. As mentioned previously, youth football was always a favourite of mine as the parents typically attend all the games. Also, any social media posts of children in football shirts after the game would be shared far and wide by the proud parents.

As another story, I was once approached by a theatre manager about sponsoring a show. Any show. We talked through how we could make this work and settled on creating a regular monthly comedy event. In return for our sponsorship money, we would be the title sponsor on the posters, flyers and tickets plus we would receive some complimentary tickets. The events were electric. The evening's compere never failed to also ridicule us gently as the sponsor in residence. Perhaps 200 people in the hall of which 50 were our guests, a group made up of customers and prospects. All 200 people knew about our business before they left at the end of the night.

There is a place for philanthropy too but in my opinion, never with totally altruistic expectations. Or rather, with planning you can be generous with your giving, but for it to still create a positive impact within your business.

In my last business, we provided each of our employees with five days per year that they could spend helping the local community or charities. We found some employees would do something unrelated to their work role as a break from their day job where others would rather stick with what they know. Where possible, a photo and story on the website blog and posted to social media provided a little more brand awareness and of course had an added benefit of reminding the rest of the team about their amazing colleagues.

9. Events

This is probably the most expensive, risky and labour-intensive marketing pillar in the list, but probably the one that could yield the best returns in the long term.

For example, if you can't find a watering hole for the sector you want to serve, you could create one. This could be a valuable conference at which you could pull together educational speakers, sponsors, exhibitors and of course the attendees who would include prospects for the services offered by the sponsors and exhibitors including you. As title sponsor, you will gain a greater profile but as I said, you will be carrying the risk.

You must measure the success of what you do across all your marketing pillars. You are particularly looking to see if something that used to resonate with your prospects is no longer interesting for them. If so, improve what you do or swap in something better. You have a finite amount of money to spend on your lead generation so spend it wisely, but make sure you spend it to avoid the need to do panic marketing 'in the trough' when your new business opportunities dry up.

Sales - New Business Process

The Why?

By this point in the book, you will have realised that much of what I believe relates to creating repeatable business processes. You will certainly have a process for handling new business today, but it may not be documented.

This chapter picks up at the point you have an enquiry and assumes you have a relationship-based business rather than a transactional business. Each of the following eight steps will need to be a repeatable process.

1. **Qualification of Enquiry**

2. **Discovery Phase**

3. **Presentation**

4. **Give Proof**

5. **Proposal**

6. **Onboarding**

7. **Get Proof**

8. **Review**

This chapter is about ensuring your new business process is both complete and consistent. Simply put, if the continued growth of your business will mean you need to recruit salespeople to your team, they are more likely to follow the process if there is a great one that is easy to follow.

Method

There is a logical flow to a great new business sales process. The quickest route from enquiry to delivery is rarely in either your or your customer's interest. Work through these process areas to explore how you can enhance what you do today to maximise the chance of success and profitable business every time.

1. Qualification of Enquiry

In the excitement of the phone ringing with a new prospect on the line, it is easy to forget that we need to first check the suitability of this enquiry. Within the foundation planning exercise at the start of this book, you defined your purpose, vision, mission and of course detailed who your avatar customer is by type, geography and size that will lead to you meeting your business growth goals.

A couple of notes to share at this point:

- There is a risk of using your marketing message to help prospects decide for themselves that they are not a great fit for you. This can result in the right prospects also not calling you, so should be avoided.

- There is a cost to you and your business of handling any new business prospect enquiry. Don't waste your time and money on opportunities that you either can't win or that you shouldn't be trying to win, because they are not aligned to your business growth goals.

Qualification can be conducted over the phone with an initial and free-flowing dialogue. Of course, you will be working from a script so you have a repeatable process, but with experience, the prospect won't feel like they are being processed.

Your script will be designed to check the alignment with your avatar. Size of business, location, alignment to how you engage, budget, timing and decision-making authority.

If a prospect at the end of this qualification step just wants you to "send me a price', you are probably not going to win any business here. Unless you have the simplest of business models, you won't have understood their pain yet.

If the enquiry qualifies as a prospect, the final step will be to agree on a date for the discovery phase. I prefer these to be done on-site with any of the key stakeholders present but with planning, you may be able to handle these via a web conference call, but don't try and complete it as part of the qualification call.

2. Discovery Phase

Handled well, this is the most valuable piece of the new business sales process. Without wishing to overstate it, I believe this stage is where new business opportunities are won or lost. Interestingly from my experience, typically this stage is rushed, but the value comes from slowing it down. Don't assume to know about the customers 'pain' even if your extensive experience means that you probably know.

As part of this discovery phase, you should complete any online research and credit checking before you go to the site just in case what you learn helps you tailor the next meeting to be more meaningful.

Like the previous qualification stage, this meeting can be handled as a script. In fact, for my last business, I created a fact-finding document with questions and spaces for the salesman to record the answers. This worked for many reasons.

- It slowed the meeting down.
- It ensured no important areas of questions were skipped.
- It kept the salesman in control of the situation.
- But it ensured that the prospect had plenty of opportunities to speak.

When I first introduced my 'needs analysis' script into our new business process, our salesman was concerned that prospects would not want to invest the time to share details of their pain. What he discovered was that prospects love to be able to tell people their tales of woe, especially if they feel that by doing so they stand a greater chance of having their issues resolved.

This was confirmed when a new customer said, "I also invited three of your competitors to quote, but you and your company were the only ones who were interested in me". As such, a tip for this stage, get to see the prospect as quickly as you can. Take biscuits along and drink lots of tea. When a person has invested this time in your relationship you will likely find they will reduce the number of your competitors they want to also spend this time with.

Before you leave this meeting, arrange for the next meeting so you can have your turn to talk when you present your solution.

To help you create your discovery phase document as part of this process, I would be pleased to share my original questionnaire via the downloads available at:

www.garethjohns.co.uk/bbb

3. Presentation

Having conducted the discovery phase, you now understand what matters to your new prospect. This meeting is your chance to confirm that what you will be proposing matches their expectations, what they value and addresses what they fear. Your presentation should talk directly about what you learned. Yes, there is a little more work to prepare, but the chances are however that it is just a tweak or two to reuse the language that they used in your discovery meeting, so they feel you have identified with their needs.

Again, I believe that these presentations are best delivered in person. Emailing a document or even a link to a video of you talking about your solution is nothing in comparison to using the emotional equity you built up by your investment in the first meeting with the prospect.

For us, we liked this second meeting to be scheduled at our own offices, so we could use this interaction to show the prospect a little of our capability, ethos and culture. Of course, it was also an opportunity to introduce key colleagues.

This meeting is not to present your proposal, but to confirm that what you plan to include in your proposal will meet the prospects expectations. This meeting will also serve to excite your prospect about the pain-free future you are promising.

Close this meeting with the agreed next steps. When can they expect the proposal from you and what is their timing for the next steps once they have received it?

4. Give Proof

The next step is to proactively introduce prospects to happy customers. If you have delivered similar projects where you have taken away the pain, share those testimonials or case study documents. Actively brokering conversations between existing customers (raving fans obviously) and new prospects at the right point in the sales process can help show who you are. Prospects love to know they are not 'patient number one', so this social proof reassures them they are with the right people and you are aligned to their needs.

As a quick story, I am currently looking to replace our rotten wooden windows with aluminium double-glazed windows. As part of the short-listing process, I am eliminating any company that only has pictures of 'traditional' white uPVC windows on their website. They may say 'We can install aluminium' but do they have any experience of doing this type of work. I don't want to learn the hard way that they want to break into this market and find that a job that's important to me, is the first one they deliver.

5. Proposal

There is a whole chapter coming up on creating winning proposals but the important point to note here within the process is that you need to ensure before you submit your proposal that you have clarity about the prospects expected timescale, being clear about the agreed next steps and the suggested timing should they agree to proceed with your proposal.

6. Onboarding

When you sign up a new customer, you are given a chance to wow them. To produce the best process here you need to put yourself in your new customer's shoes and think from their perspective what would make the relationship successful. The following list won't apply to all business types but may help your thinking process as you produce your list.

- Create a new customer in your internal systems.
- Advise your team about the new customer, their pain and your promises.
- Introduce your key people to their key people.
- Attend the customers next team meeting to explain what you will be doing for them and by when. Manage their expectations. If applicable, share the goals or targets you will be held to.
- Following the team meeting, provide written guidance to the new customer's team on what they can expect from you and how to contact you.
- Make it memorable. Celebrate the new partnership and impress them.

7. Get Proof

Just after onboarding is the right time to gain testimonials, Google reviews or request that your new customer will work with you on the creation of more detailed case studies. If in section 4 you gave proof to your new customer, they will be expecting you to ask and be pleased to help you. This section of your process also keeps your bank of proof for reuse current.

8. Review

Excellence comes from continual business process improvement. It's worth having a plan to revisit this new business process at least annually, but initially at least quarterly to ensure that it's all working and being used by your team as you expect.

Sales - Pre-Sales Process

The Why?

Whether what you sell is bespoke or a standardised repeatable offering, there is a role for a pre-sales function. For clarity, I will call everything that you deliver to a customer a 'project'.

Salespeople love to sell and typically this process starts with selling the dream. When the dream becomes a proposal and the customer agrees to it, there can be a gap between the dream and reality that ends in customer dissatisfaction.

So, what do I mean by pre-sales?

In its simplest term, what you are looking to achieve is a level of buy-in from the members of your team who deliver the project in support of the efforts of the sales team. Yes, this means allowing people who get paid to deliver to invest some time before the sale, but that will result in a better outcome after the sale. For smaller businesses pre-sales is an additional function of one or more of the delivery team. As the need increases this could end up as a whole job on its own, but you would probably pull someone from the delivery team to fill the role to ensure that you always benefit from that perspective.

Topics that the pre-sales role should be considering include:

1. Suitability
2. Time & Resources
3. Costs
4. Sanity

Finally, there are some additional benefits of formalising a pre-sales role within your organisation for the delivery of your projects, which include accuracy, customers perception of your business, a point of difference from your competition and a sense of teamwork.

Method

There is a risk that the quality of project delivery is dependent on the person doing the delivery having the ability to problem solve the challenges as they run into them. With planning, lots of those challenges could have been foreseen and as such, avoided with planning. This in turn means your choice of employees to deliver projects becomes wider than your number one problem solver.

Your pre-sales process will include these four elements.

1. Suitability

Will this project deliver against the dream the salesperson sold? This is also where you would be checking the specification details. Does what you are proposing work with everything the customer already has? What is the future roadmap for the solution you are providing? Is this a good long term solution for the customer? How long before what you are selling or expecting your solution to work with will become obsolete?

2. Time & Resources

How much time do you need to deliver this solution? This may also include working out how much can be prepared offsite before you spend any time with the client. Do you have the team resources and cash flow for materials for this project? How much of the solution can be delivered by lower-skilled or augmented labour?

3. Costs

Now you have finalised the specifications, the time required (at your regular day and out of hours rates) and what resources you need to deliver the solution, you can provide details of the costs and scope of works to the salesperson to create their proposal. Because pre-sales are aligned to delivery rather than sales, it's in their interest to get these figures to be accurate and deliverable.

4. Sanity

The pre-sales function is also another pair of eyes to look at the solution proposed. This ensures it's more than just the salesman that believes the proposal to be the right solution for the customer and your business.

As mentioned in the opening of this chapter there are some additional benefits of resourcing a pre-sales function within your business and understanding these will help you realise why you are going to put the investment in time creating the role.

- **Accuracy** - Right first time. This of course represents a cost-saving to the business because you can more quickly move onto the next project and not end up with incorrectly ordered materials or items missing from sales invoices. You can also schedule your projects closer together, leaving less wasteful contingency time. If the pre-sales team say it will take 4-days to deliver, you can more safely book just the required 4-days.

- **Perception -** The customer will love that you have a process to ensure they are getting the best solution to their challenge. In a sales role, don't demonise the fact that you can't quote until pre-sales have reviewed the project but help the customer understand why this step creates more accurate and aligned projects.

- **Difference** - In a crowded marketplace, this could be a difference that you can highlight to your prospects. Why should they deal with you? Because you have a pre-sales process. Having a pre-sales process reminds the customer that they are buying the services of a team. A kind of reminder that what you deliver requires a wide skillset.

- **Team -** The old saying that the team is only as strong as the weakest player is especially true when it comes to delivering projects. Having a pre-sales function uses the right technical resources in the precise place that will ensure the success of delivery. This will encourage the team to work together with the common aim being the delivery of projects that drive customer satisfaction and come in on budget.

Pre-sales could be a single person but think of it as a role that you could have several people cover, whilst you ensure enough time is allocated for the level of project work you have. This could become a full-time role, but until then ensure that anyone covering this role works to the same standard. Using the same process.

An hour invested in pre-sales is probably equivalent to five hours of avoided remedial work and apologies given to the customer or even worse, compensation payments being demanded.

Sales - Proposals

The Why?

We need to start this chapter by thinking about why we document a proposal, when we should submit and how we should present it. We also need to cover why some business owners claim to only win 1 in 3 deals and others win a massive 2 out of 3 deals (When you think about the maths, that's 100% more wins!). Importantly, you need to consider what should be included in your proposal.

The purpose of a proposal is not just to give a price, but also to confirm what you will be delivering for that price. The most successful proposals focus on why the buyer will be better off for signing on the dotted line rather than the costs and raw specification details.

There is a cost and risk to producing a good proposal. Before you start your process, it is worth ensuring there is a real business need and budget for your proposal. From my experience, if you are not close enough to the prospect to learn these two facts, you won't win the business either. You also may not be talking to the decision-maker for your proposal which is not a problem, but you do need to ascertain who will be making the decision and when it will be made before you start this process.

As far as presenting your proposal, in person always felt to me like a connection was being made. Of course, since the 2020 pandemic caused a change of mindset about remote working, in person also includes video conference calls. If you believe in what you are delivering, that will shine through and the prospect will buy into your enthusiasm. The instances of customers who say "Just send me a quote" going forward to buy has always been low. Again, not a hard rule but check your success history. Also, if the buying decision is not being made by your contact, having the chance to present it to the decision-maker is a reasonable request.

Your proposal should include these eight elements:

1. Statement of need
2. Recommended solution
3. Scope of works
4. Price
5. Options
6. Capability and capacity
7. Specification
8. Legal

Method

I enjoy receiving great sales proposals, but they are rare. Use the tips in this chapter to improve your proposals, so they stand out from whatever your competitors submit. Rarely are proposals printed now, so don't scrimp on the page count but consider readability and impact as your top goals.

Following on from the **Sales – New Business Process** chapter, proposals are only sent to firm up what you have already discussed with the prospect or customer. But that firming up is also your last chance to impress your contact at the client's business. This is however also your first and only chance to impress others who may read the proposal and influence the decision. Your proposal document could be much more important than perhaps you have previously given it credit.

These eight elements are shown here in a specific order. Some people have an opinion that you should carry a one-page executive summary at the front allowing a busy reader to get to 'the price' without needing to worry about what's included or importantly, excluded. I don't believe this to be good practice. By helping a busy reader get to the page with the price on via a contents page, they at least know they are choosing to skip important pages so they can own their lack of comprehension.

1. Statement of need

Restate what you were asked to solve and the current pain using as much of the language as they used when they told you about it. This could be no more than a couple of paragraphs but give it a page of its own. It's that important.

2. Recommended solution

You have already talked this through with your contact at the client, but this is where you need to provide an executive summary covering a succinct list of the benefits of your proposed and recommended solution.

3. Scope of works

You need to be clear on what is included and importantly what is excluded from this proposal. For example, if it doesn't include the cost of removing any waste, make sure that is clear. The more effort you put into the scope of works, which will come from your pre-sales activity, the more likely when you win the proposal you will be able to deliver it accurately, on time, on budget and matching the client's expectations.

4. Price

Clarity is everything here too. I recommend providing enough detail of the materials for the client to be sure of the quality of what you are providing.

I remember losing an order in my IT business where the customer told me when they later returned to us, "Well, you both quoted for HP servers so I went with the cheapest". The issue caused by me and ultimately a problem for my ex-customer was that I was selling a high-end server and the competitor won the work by selling a low-spec server and the customer couldn't tell the difference.

As a tip, if you can, move away from an hourly rate proposal to a project price. The problem with hourly rate proposals is the customer expects it to be a worst-case price. If you finish the project earlier, you will charge them less but if it takes longer, that's your problem. With hourly rate proposals, you as the supplier can be the only loser.

Lastly, this section needs to include your payment terms. Don't be shy to ask for deposits or even pre-payment, especially in unknown relationships.

5. Options

The main specification and price in section 4 will need to be enough to deliver against the customer's objectives and something you will be pleased to deliver. As in, don't deliberately reduce the specification and price in section 4 just to get the work if it's beneath your minimum specification or quality point as that will backfire on you.

However, as mentioned in the products and services chapter, up to 20% of customers will be willing to pay for a premium option. That's one out of five of your proposals that could be enhanced with some optional upgrades. Of course, that statistic only works if you create premium upgrade options and include them within the proposal.

For any suggested optional upgrades include both the cost impact and any additional benefits they will gain. If it is advantageous to agree to this option at the same time as the main project, ensure you mention those benefits too.

Be careful not to include too many options as it is known that if there are too many options where customers are expected to think, they often end up choosing nothing at all. This is sometimes called analysis paralysis. In the automotive world, they tend to bundle options together into group packs such as the 'sound pack' or 'comfort pack' to make decision making easier.

6. Capability and capacity

Assuming this is not the first time you have delivered a proposal like this, within this section, show the proof of your previous work. Testimonials, photographs, case studies or details of references who would be pleased to vouch for your capability.

If you have qualifications or certifications to deliver your services, this is the place within the proposal to provide details of those too.

Subtly, what you are doing in this section by providing this information is helping to shine a light on what may be missing from your competitor's proposals and perhaps missing from their business.

7. Specification

As your document continues you will have fewer readers left as their need for information has been addressed. This section is all about 'speeds-and-feeds'. The details of the project you will be delivering.

Depending on your sector this could be the specification of the paint coating, the speed of the fan or the type of fabric you will use. This is also where you can provide details of any third-party providers that will be handling any warranty work for your solution or underwritten guarantees.

It's better to include the content in this section than to be asked for it afterwards, seeming like you were trying to hide details of the project. Although the first proposals may take some time to create, the paragraphs you include in this section will quickly become standard elements that you can pull from to assemble a proposal.

8. Legal

Everyone loves terms and conditions. Remember that unless you supply them as part of your proposal you can't depend on them protecting you if you end up in court so include them with every proposal.

Sales - Account Management

The Why

It's commonly understood that it typically costs at least five times as much to get a new customer as it costs to retain an existing one. By extension therefore your customer retention efforts should at least be given a budget, which could easily be one-fifth of what you spend on your marketing and new business growth investment.

However, the benefits of an amazing account management process include more than the lack of customers leaving you, ultimately to be serviced by your competitors. As you read the rest of this chapter, you will I am sure be increasing the priority, attention and budget that this process is given in your business.

So, let's explore what's going on in a business today that doesn't have an effective account management process.

- **Only the squeaky wheels** – Please excuse the Americanism, but the squeaky wheel gets the grease. It's not unusual for only the loudest or largest customers to get any strategic attention from your limited account management resource.

- **Fear of awakening the beast** – If you engage with the customers about how they interact with you today, they may realise that you don't do much for the money you charge.

- **Lack of resource** – You believe that one size should fit all because you like things fitting neatly into boxes. You don't have the resource to look after all your customers in the way you would like, so as of today, you don't try.

- **Nothing to say** – You don't believe you have anything of value to tell the customer so you don't go to see them and as such, you also miss the opportunity to listen to them too.

- **Social proof** – Getting reviews onto Google or gaining referrals from your existing customers feels unnatural and uncomfortable.

This chapter will provide you with the top ten fundamentals of a great account management process. How many of these are your current process delivering for your business consistently?

Method

The lack of a documented and repeatable account management process won't cause immediate problems for your business. You can probably go for years just being reactive to your customer's needs. Sadly, however, a model without effective account management doesn't scale well. When a customer leaves you stating "You have grown so much that we no longer feel important" what they are saying is that your account management process has let them down.

The top ten account management fundamentals are as follows.

1. Clarity

It's important to start with clarity of why you want to have an account management process. Ensure there is buy-in, especially from the leadership and sales teams that are likely to be delivering this process.

- Improving and then maintaining customer relationships.
- A better understanding of your customer's needs.
- Educating your customers about what is possible.
- Helping customers strategically set their investment budgets.
- Potentially a marketable competitive point of difference.

2. Training

During the start-up phase for most businesses, the founders will be the principal sales and account management resources. The handover to employees who have been recruited for this role requires a repeatable training process and the great news is that these are skills that can be learned.

What does a recruit need to know to be able to do an amazing job of delivering an effective account management process?

3. Categorising customers

Typically, the customers of most businesses will be a mixed group, with varying needs, demands and available budgets. However, it's not unusual for business owners to try and introduce a one-size-fits-all approach to account management.

The alternative is to design an account management process that is tailored to your client base. Typically, I find that three groups work here.

- **Proactive Customers** – This group of customers spend on your services because they need what you do and they look to you to advise them about investing and support them in their buying decisions. You can plan your business around these mature customers' needs and their planned and budgeted spending.

- **Reactive Customers** – The second group reluctantly spend because they must, so it's a less predictable income stream but you need your reactive process to capture the opportunities when they arise. They are still loyal to your business.

- **Reluctant Customers** – At the bottom of this categorisation list are the customers who don't have much money to spend and probably never will. They will always shop around and only buy from you because they have no other choice.

Unless you have been very careful who you sign up as customers, it's not unusual for the proactive customers to only account for about 20% of your customer base, but they will be generating 80% of your revenue and profits. This commonly found phenomenon is called the Pareto Principle.

There is a cost to delivering account management, but with this categorisation completed you now know that you should be focussing most of your efforts on the top 20% of your customers.

4. Key account managers

Your sector and customer needs are likely to dictate how many account managers you need. In the IT sector, I found that once an account manager has more than about 20 customers to look after the quality of the relationships fell away dramatically especially because the processes that we operated included going to the site to meet with the customers.

5. Budget setting

There is a feeling that talking about money is somehow vulgar, but it's even worse if you surprise a customer with a capital cost need that you could foresee but didn't talk to the customer about it.

Think about your best customer and what you supply to them today. What will they need from you in the next 12 months? What will they then need next year and the year after? Document this with enough narrative for them to understand why this should be in their budget. Will they need to upgrade or invest in newer versions of what you supply for them to remain competitive? Your proactive customer's group will love this type of help.

When the next financial year starts, you are not going to be fighting for budget because it has already been reserved for your proposed projects.

6. Business reviews

By this stage in the ten fundamentals, you have shortlisted the accounts you are going to manage, assigned an account manager and worked out what they need to be spending in future. You now need a process to conduct a regular meaningful business review.

A great business review will include discussions around:

- Your performance in the delivery of the services they purchase from you.
- Customer satisfaction
- Future strategic project planning.
- Budget planning.

Meet too frequently and you will be seen as a time nuisance. Too infrequently and you may as well not have an account management process. Quarterly works for most sectors, but some customers may need to see you monthly. It's fine to create a rhythm that suits your proactive customer's needs. Without them, you don't have a business anyway!

Reactive customers typically won't understand the benefits of your account management process but will have your help in defining a one-off project during which you will need to learn all you can to enable you to help define the project.

7. Relationships

Building meaningful relationships comes out of caring authentically for your customers as individuals and their businesses. I know this could appear to be insincere, but sometimes to make this a habit you may need to remind yourself to be nice.

Set time aside to think about what you can do to help your customers and their businesses. Information you can send them that would be useful to them or sometimes just a relevant joke. Take the time to read their social posts and comment or like them.

Make the effort to be part of their life, which will help you increase emotional capital and their trust in you.

8. Social proof

With all the effort invested in creating great relationships, you can leverage them to your advantage. You will find that when you approach customers who are actively account managed from your 'Proactive Customers' group you will find they will be pleased to help you.

That could include co-written case studies, providing testimonials or acting as a reference. Importantly though, because of how well you know this group of customers you can make your request meaningful to generate the documents you need for your library. If they help you out and you want to give them an impromptu gift to say thank you, you can also make that relevant for them. No point in giving a great bottle of wine as a thank you to someone who is teetotal!

9. Cross-selling opportunities

The easiest sales you can make are of a product you already sell to a customer with whom you have an existing relationship. It still surprises me that this is often overlooked.

Ignore the opportunity to cross-sell at your peril. If this lack of attention continues for too long, often the customers' need for the other services you could sell, but don't often talk about, end up being served by your competitors. Before you know it, they are no longer your customer for any of your services.

Cross-selling is therefore not an opportunity, but a critical necessity.

10. Performance and rewards

Everything in business can be measured, but you need to be careful to measure the right things. In the case of account management, I believe you need to measure a mixture of activities and outcomes.

You may want to measure the percentage of qualifying accounts for a proactive account management process that enjoyed time with their account manager. This is an activity.

It will also be worth measuring how many of the proactive accounts have strategic budgets in place. Again, this is an activity but without outline budgets in place, you won't feel the benefit of this investment.

Finally, you will want to measure the performance somehow. For me, I like to measure the cross-sales activity (sales to proactive customers of things you already sell to others). This helps you see the return on your investment in account management resource.

Putting it all into a repeatable process

My advice here is to start with your view of an optimum process and try and put that in place for all your proactive clients. If some of those customers want to meet their account managers more often, this is never a bad thing.

One last tip is to keep the process dynamic. A few small enhancements in your process and reporting each year will keep it interesting for your customers and your account managers.

Sales - Pricing Strategy

The Why?

When I was young and naive, I believed that if I sold something for more than I paid for it, I had a successful business. There was very little more science in it than that. This method of operation produced irregular and inconsistent results for years, but during that time I didn't realise why.

No matter your level of interest in improving your understanding of finance, this chapter will give you a good insight to help you better understand from the sales value down through the variable cost of goods, gross profit, fixed operating costs, finally arriving at net profit.

With a pricing strategy, you will find creating new services and products both easier and more likely to be in line with the rest of your offering. There is a minimum price you can afford to sell at and this will help you find that. Once you have that true cost price in mind you can work on creating your selling price that is in line with the market and your customer's pocket.

Once you have a formula for calculating sales values that will drive a consistent retained net profit, the next topic you need to understand in this chapter is discounting. There are massive customer value perception risks to discounting in addition to losing your profit margin. Strategies for both are covered in this chapter.

Method

I realise that many readers will have a great financial understanding but this chapter is for anyone that needs to understand more or would like a refresher. This starts with a reminder of five important terms.

- **Sales Revenue** – The invoice value of your goods and services.

- **Cost of Goods** – These costs are directly related to the delivery of the sale. This will include the purchase of raw materials and the labour costs to deliver your services. These are known as variable costs.

- **Gross Profit** – Deduct the **Cost of Goods** from the **Sales Revenue**.

- **Direct Costs** – These are the purchases for everything else. Sales, admin and management labour, marketing, office space, insurance, telephones. In general, these costs don't change much if your sales revenue changes so they are known as fixed costs.

- **Net Profit** – This is what you have left after you deduct the **Direct Costs** from the **Gross Profit**.

If today you consider all your labour to be a direct cost, ensure this is the right decision. In the IT Services sector, for example, all engineering resource is considered a cost of goods. If you don't provide any services, you don't need any engineers. They are a variable cost.

To improve your business profitability, start with the gross profit.

There are three options to improve the **Gross Profit** of your business.

1. **Sell more** (either more often or to more customers)
2. **Sell for more** (increase your unit selling price)
3. **Buy cheaper** (reduce your cost of goods – materials or labour efficiency)

Review the services you offer

What does it cost you today to deliver each of your services? You know the selling price, but what are the variable costs attached at an individual service level? As in, each £100 of sales revenue is not likely to contribute the same amount to your business profitability. Be honest here regarding all the labour costs that go into your sale.

Are all your services profitable? If not, can you increase the selling price (option 2) or reduce the costs (option 3) to make the gross profitability better? The reason I am labouring this point is that if you opted for sell more (option 1) without checking the profitability and the service is already not profitable, selling more of it will only make your trading position worse. Secondly. Although reducing the costs (option 3) could fix the profitability right now, you can't expect to save costs again in future years. At some point, you will have to increase your price.

Depending on your sector there is probably an expected level of gross profit. The IT Services industry runs at about 50% gross profit. So, if a service costs £150 to deliver it should be sold at £300.

Premium Services

As I mentioned in the Products & Services Offering chapter of this book, for most sectors about 20% of customers would be willing to consider a premium option but of course, only if you have a premium option to offer them.

The key takeaway here is that your premium service should bring at least the same level of gross profit percentage to your business. Ideally, it may even be a more profitable service if you can sell it based on the value it will bring to your customer rather than the cost you will incur to deliver it. Of course, you need to know what it will cost to deliver the premium service before you can decide the cost for your new service.

Pricing Increases

Customers cope better with the news that you intend to put your prices up a small amount each year rather than a big amount every five years. Your business costs will increase every year, so ensure you review your sales prices at least annually too. Everyone else who is consistently profitable already does this.

The Danger of Discounting

When you run a promotion that includes a discount on your sales it feels like you are offering a discount off the retail price that you show the customer, but it's critical to understand that the first money you are giving away is at the bottom line.

Let's assume for the following example that a business usually makes a gross profit of 65% and a net profit of 15%. Therefore, using nice round numbers let's assume a sale of £100. It will cost £35 to deliver the sale (leaving 65% gross profit) and will carry £50 of your fixed costs, leaving £15 of net profit.

Building on that model, let's think about gambling that giving 10% off your services will drive additional sales, but it only generating about the same volume of sales.

	Normal Sale	10% Discount
Sales Revenue	£100	£100
Discount Percentage		10%
Discount Amount		£10
Cost of Goods	**£35**	**£35**
Gross Profit	£65 (65%)	£55 (55%)
Direct Costs	**£50**	**£50**
Net Profit	£15 (15%)	£5 (5%)

Because you don't have additional sales revenue, your direct costs of £50 per £100 of sale will remain. The outcome of a 10% discount would be that your bottom-line net profit would only be £5 rather than £15. You would therefore need to sell three times as much just to equal your old level of net profitability.

The next question you would then need to answer is about your direct costs. If you sell three times as much, will you need more sales or administrative staff or a bigger office to work from etc? If so, that £50 per £100 of sales value may even increase.

The last two considerations on this topic are:

- What does it look like to your customers and prospects if you always offer discounts? Is your pricing model encouraging your customers to defer their purchase until your next sale?
- Larger customers often expect lower prices, but often their requirements are more complex and their need to be looked after comes at a greater cost to you. You don't want to be doing more work for less money, which is typically the outcome of discounting the unit price for larger customers.

Delivery - Project Management

The Why?

For clarity, when I say 'Project Management' in this chapter, I am talking about the projects you deliver to your clients. Today you may just call them orders, irrespective of whether it's a large or small amount of work. Having a process for project management will create ownership and accountability.

Without project management, your projects can derail with the finger of blame being pointed in all directions. The frequently used phrase 'one throat to choke', only shows us the negative side of the accountability that comes with ensuring there is ownership of projects.

Think instead about the phrase 'one hand to shake'. By this, I don't mean one hand for you to shake, but one hand for the customer to shake. Somebody who owns the positive outcome of the project.

Within this chapter we will discuss:

- Communication
- The Glue
- Remedial Activity
- Improved Cash Flow
- Case Studies
- Chargeable Service

The purpose of project management is to ensure all projects are completed profitably, on time whilst creating satisfied customers.

Method

The problem with any task being everyone's responsibility is that its relevance and urgency is not always felt by everyone, or in some cases by anyone. Project Management should therefore be a role and if you have enough project work, it may be something you employ someone specifically for. This chapter focuses on creating the role and the scope of what you are looking to achieve in the first instance.

Communication

One of the biggest frustrations for customers is not knowing. It could be not knowing when you will start, when you will finish or what they can or can't use, whilst you are doing your work. The management of your customer expectations starts with having a continuous open dialogue between the customer and someone within your organisation. The actions of your Project Manager will reassure the customer that your company is in control.

When a new project is created, your Project Manager will contact the customer to let them know what to expect and how to contact them with any queries. If the customer responds better to meetings in person, the Project Manager should be ready to do that.

The Glue

When a new project is created there is a list of materials, a scope of works and some ideas of when the work needs to happen. The Project Manager needs to sanity check the project and then arrange all the resources to be available at the right time to ensure successful delivery. They will also report back the financial outcomes of projects which will help the pre-sales team continually improve their ability to create accurate proposals.

Remedial Activity

Having a Project Manager working closely with the customer creates a relationship of value. This is especially useful should there be any challenges during your project delivery where you may need to depend on the emotional capital created as the Project Manager proactively handles any remedial works.

Improved Cash Flow

Typically, you will only get paid the balance of any project once the project is complete. Open projects that have not yet been signed off by the customer because of some niggling final actions cause cash flow issues. Having a Project Manager who understands this means you should be able to close projects quicker leading to improved cash flow.

Case Studies

The customer and Project Manager will be able to share the pride of getting to project completion. The Project Manager is in the right place to ensure the customer actively participates in the creation of a case study. Make it part of your process as this will drive future sales.

Chargeable Service

The work of the Project Manager should be a chargeable service given how crucial it is to success. Depending on your sector it could be that you won't show it as a line on the proposal but will load the labour costs for this into the total project costs.

Take these six elements and design your step by step process for project management in your business. Then see who within your team has the required people and analytical skills to take on this role and allocate them time accordingly.

Delivery - Measurement

The Why?

I mentioned earlier in this book Peter Drucker's quote 'What you measure gets managed!', but this is just the start of the challenge. What happens if you measure the wrong thing?

The big question here is should you measure the **input** or activity effort being put into the task at hand, or the **output** or performance of that task. The unhelpful answer is that it depends! By this I mean it depends on what you are going to do with the data you collect. It's worth also noting that most input metrics are typically leading current data and outputs are often trailing historical data.

Let's consider a telesales example. We think that if one salesman makes 500 phone calls in a week, they will generate 5 (1%) qualified enquiries. At some point, those 5 enquiries will become one sale.

From this example, the 500 phone calls are the input **activity**. The 5 qualified enquiries are the output **performance** of that role. This chapter will discuss why you should measure both the inputs and the outputs, and why you should only reward the outputs. You will notice that I have not suggested we do anything with the actual sales that may or may not come from this activity, because it is not in the control of that employee.

How you reward performance may impact behaviour. For example, if you reward an individual's performance only, what impact could that have on their commitment to their part in the team. The best reward schemes give sufficient thought to how the employee may try and game the system for their benefit.

As a summary, this chapter will cover why everyone needs to own their numbers, the creation of an accountability chart and the difference between input and output metrics.

Method

Often business owners only start to measure performance when things are not going well to try to get their poorly performing staff to improve or provide the reasons to move them on. My proposal with this chapter is to fix the issue of performance before you have an issue with performance. A kind of way to manage the expectations of everyone in your company.

Everyone Needs To Own Their Number

My experience is that employees like to feel that their contribution is valuable to the success of the business. But often the contribution of individuals is lost into the aggregated whole. Does everyone in your team today have clarity of what good looks like specifically for their role? How many widgets do they need to make, or how many phone calls they should take? If today you don't have a performance issue all you need to do is measure what everyone does. Voilà!

The Accountability Chart

For every role within your company, there are probably 4-6 headline activities. Each of those will have its definition of what good looks like. Taking the time to document each of these will provide clarity for the employee who takes on that role.

The headings for your chart should include:

- **Activity** – A descriptive title for the activity.
- **The 'Why'** – The reason this activity needs to be done, summarised in a paragraph or two.
- **Key Activity Indicator** – This is the 'input' work the employee will need to do to deliver against this activity. There can be numbers in here, but often you don't need them.
- **Key Performance Indicator** – And this is the number that matters as it's the 'output'.
- **What Good Looks Like** – This is a paragraph detailing the 'feeling' that will come from this activity being delivered well.
- **Call for help** – The final optional heading is to help the rest of the team understand what they can do to help the owner of this activity achieve success in their role.

There is an example Accountability Chart as an Excel file that you can download from my website at www.garethjohns.co.uk/bbb

I would like at this point to introduce you to some terms you can use in measuring activity and performance, arranged neatly into an easy-to-understand pyramid.

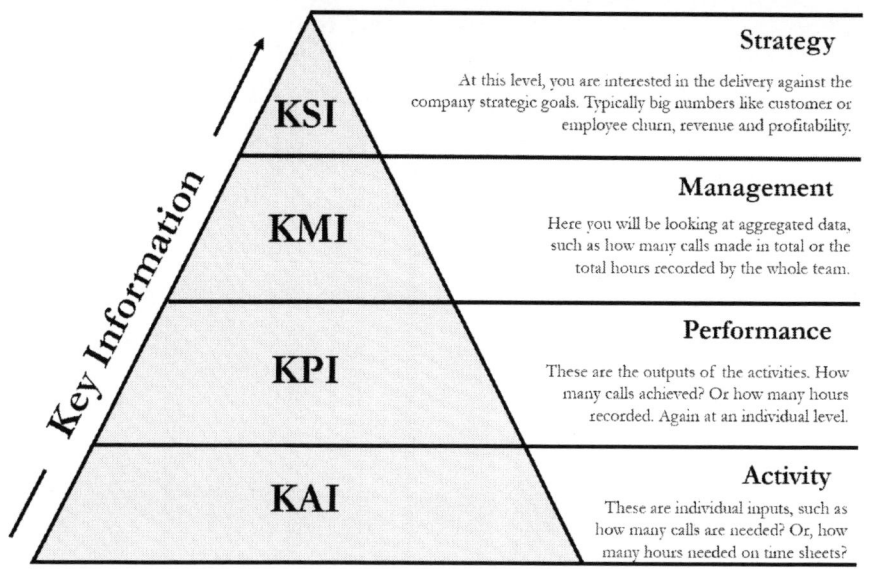

Often people talk about KPI's to mean all measured numbers, but I find it helpful to have specific terms to describe the aggregated data.

- **Key Performance Information** – At an individual contribution level, every activity will have an input (KAI) and a performance output (KPI). Yes, you can then use the numbers to highlight non-performers, but this is also useful for employees to be able to see if their performance meets or even exceeds the company's expectations.

- **Key Management Information** – At this level of aggregation you should be looking at the total achievement of any teams. How many units were made today by the team? How many dinners were served? These will always be outputs rather than inputs and this is the level that your team leaders should focus on.

- **Key Strategic Information** – Again, these will be performance-based numbers but will be limited to just those numbers that indicate how aligned you are to your strategic goals. If you are looking for 15% business growth this year, that's probably not a bad performance metric to monitor. Maybe you know that you will only achieve that level of growth if your customer satisfaction is more than 80%, so that may be a good trailing statistic to measure too.

Rewarding Performance

The final part of this chapter is around using numbers to help you calculate performance bonuses. As per the **People - Pay Structure** chapter in this book, everyone in the company should be paid a base wage for turning up to work and then both a performance-based bonus (based on their KPIs) and then either a team or companywide bonus based on the KMI figures.

When you design a rewarding pay structure based on performance, model what would happen to the compensation if an individual employee drastically under or over-performs. Would there be a potential knock-on impact on the morale of their team colleagues? Once you get your structure right, it will both motivate and reward the right behaviours to bring business success.

Delivery - Root Cause Analysis

The Why?

The things we plan to happen don't always turn out the way we hoped, but on the condition that we learn something from the experience, it's still an investment in our skills. The author Daniel Pink talks about our need in business, not for problem solvers, but problem finders. That's kind of amusing when we spend so much time praising the members of our team who are good at solving problems but see those that find problems as a nuisance because they cause us extra work.

This chapter is all about the creation of workarounds. In average businesses, when your team stumble into a challenge they find a workaround, the customer is happy and you move on to the next project. Successful businesses realise that workarounds although a necessity within the moment, is just the start of the journey to business improvement, rather than the end.

What you need is to create a process whereby you capture the workarounds to be reviewed in detail so you can consider if you could change the outcome should it happen again. That's the critical part of this. You can't impact the last time it happened, but what would the team do if it happened again? Or even better, what can you do to stop the challenge from ever happening again?

As part of this review process, you also must consider if it is a unicorn issue where the chances of it happening again are incredibly slim and in which case it may need no more of your time. At least you gave it some consideration.

Importantly, you are not going to stop the workarounds within the moment as those are often part of what drives customer satisfaction. You and your team will still get on and fix the challenge.

To give you further reason to spend the time creating a process, let me give you a real-world example:

In my former life as an owner of an IT support business, we used to handle an inordinate amount of password change support requests. For years we just got on and helped the customer get reconnected. It was only once we applied this process, we realised we had done woefully little to teach our customers how to manage their password reset. We created some teaching materials and actively pushed this out to all the users creating a massive decrease in support tickets, which saved us time and of course, allowed the users to spend more time in their role.

Method

There is a quote that is commonly attributed to Albert Einstein that reads, "The definition of insanity is doing the same thing over and over again and expecting a different result.". Allowing workarounds to deal with challenges without looking to find what is the root cause of the challenge is therefore insanity.

We believe it's better to stop drugs coming into the country and to teach our children right from wrong and that they should eat their greens. Our understanding of these topics and their subsequent resolutions at the root of the issues are designed to stop us as a society from having issues with drugs, crime and poor health.

This process comes with a five-step plan. Work through them in order.

Step One – Where do the workarounds happen in your business?

This may be the toughest step to take, depending on how much data you collect about the actions of your team and the satisfaction of your customers. Sometimes the workarounds are hidden from managers. The employees just do what they need to do to keep the customer happy. Start by trawling over your customer feedback to see which things look to be causing the most upset. Check the projects that took longer than expected or required too many trips to the customer site and ask the questions why. This may reveal where workarounds are being put into place. Importantly you are looking for trends and not isolated mistakes.

Initially, there may be limited trust in this process from your team and a fear that what you will uncover will have repercussions. What if the workarounds you discover were not completed the way you would have done? Ensure your language and behaviour reassures your team that this is to make a better process for the future.

Step Two – Create a mechanism to capture workarounds as they happen?

From your initial investigation, you now know what a workaround looks like. Create a process for your team to be able to flag when they have had to go to the site twice, use more materials than expected or apologise to the customer. This could be a form, an email template or even a post-it note. Whatever will work best for your team.

The team needs to know that this process is all about continual improvement. Yes, of course, you need to perform an autopsy of sorts on the workaround delivered to understand the cause but ensure this is never considered a personal affront.

Step Three – Creating the workarounds team who will own this process

From experience, the best team for this process will come from across the breadth of your organisation. You want to create a team of about four people. I always see the value of having someone with a finance head in these teams so they can bring the reality about just how much money you waste on your workarounds. You are looking for people who are analytical but also not afraid to question the status quo! You can use this to develop next-generation leaders, but always ensure it's a mixed team including one of your newest recruits. They are more likely to say, "I don't understand why we do this?"

You may want to keep the team fresh by allowing members to be swapped out perhaps on a 12-month tenure but ideally don't swap everyone out the same month, so you can keep the momentum of the team.

Step Four – Agree on a schedule and structure for the group's meetings

For most businesses, this is probably a half-day per month time investment. It is reasonable to expect the group to report back their work too so you can see that they are making progress in identifying the root cause of the workarounds and either coming up with resolutions or at least reporting back the issues so other teams can be assembled to come up with the fix. As I said at the start of this chapter, this team is about problem finders, not problem solvers!

When you get this process right you will save more money than it costs you for this group to meet, so don't obsess too much about the cost of giving this team some reserved time to work on the business.

Step Five – Educate the whole team

When an employee attends a customer's site and doesn't have the right materials for the third time this month, maybe it's the right time for the employee to flag this up to the root cause team. They may find that it's inaccurate quoting, purchasing delays, goods in not reconciling deliveries or even the employee who flagged the issue not understanding the process for going to a customer's site.

Use the success of your initial fixes to teach everyone on the team the advantages of finding the root cause of challenges. This will help them realise why it's in their interest to flag any future workarounds. Help them picture a time when all jobs run on time and within the budget which of course, will impact their bonus payments.

Delivery - Customer Satisfaction

Why?

You assume that if your customers buy from you again this month, they must be happy with you and the service you provide.

Sadly, all too often the first time you know a customer is unhappy is when they don't come back to buy again.

By this point, it's too late to retain the customer and often too late to learn anything that will increase your chances of improving your service provision.

I am sure you will agree that there is now an overload of requests for feedback and most of it seems quite inauthentic. This, I believe, is due to the sense we have that it doesn't matter how we respond, nothing changes. The service doesn't get better.

Your system for collecting customer feedback needs to be built around the value for the customer in providing a response, which means you also need to work on changing the customer's perception of why they should provide you with this essential information.

Happiness is of course subjective. The customer is always right ... about how they feel. Depending on your mood, when you are asked to complete a survey may determine how fair and reasonable your response is and it's no different for your customers. As such, you need to learn how to react to aggregated data and trends in your feedback rather than to create knee-jerk reactions to individual customer responses. Of course, this only works if you are receiving enough customer feedback for it to be meaningful.

Another advantage of collecting customer satisfaction data is that when a customer perceives that the service that they have received is below the grade they expect, you would rather know there is a mismatch between their perception and the reality so you can help them understand what they should expect.

Even with the best customer satisfaction plan, you will still churn customers for other reasons such as price, but I was always taught that customers should never leave because of service. It's even more frustrating if a customer leaves because of a misconception of what they believed should have been the service you are providing.

Method

As you create your process around measuring customer satisfaction, ensure you consider the following four steps.

1. When, How and Who?

The timing and method of asking for feedback are both important and very much depend on what you plan to do with the data.

Most feedback requests split into two types.

Relationship

This type of feedback is normally requested via a survey that allows you to ask multiple questions about your services and how the customer feels about working with your company.

This type of feedback is typically only collected once or twice per year. Typically, you would only ask the opinion of whoever is responsible for buying your services rather than the end-users who receive your services.

If you ask any more often, the customer can become bored of the process and your response rate falls.

Transactional

With this type of feedback, you would ask immediately after you deliver your service for the customer or recipient of your service to rate you. As a guide, the easier it is for the customer to give feedback, the more likely you will get enough data for it to be meaningful. As soon as you make this a detailed questionnaire, you will massively reduce the number of responses you require.

Ideally, just ask for them to click a face. Happy or sad. Maybe have a neutral face in the middle. There are platforms for most industries that enable this type of feedback collection. Often there is an optional field for the recipient to add some notes and there is magic in what they choose to tell you, good or bad!

Because this feedback is requested from the recipient of your service rather than the contact at your customer who purchased the services, the data tends to be more meaningful and useful.

A quick note about Net Promotor Scores

Often this is in the form of one question to determine loyalty which asks, "On a scale of 0-10 if asked, how likely would you recommend this company". This is called the Net Promotor Score (NPS) question, a theory created in 1996 by Fred Reichheld that has become widely used but often misunderstood. This question is often used in a transactional way but is asking about relational loyalty and I believe should be reserved for that type of feedback request.

0	1	2	3	4	5	6	7	8	9	10
			Detractors				Passives		Promoters	

The **detractors** are customers that would actively go out of their way to tell people they know why they shouldn't work with you and for the sake of your reputation, you probably shouldn't be working with them. The **passives** are a relatively quiet group but are receptive to competing offers and are where you need to focus your energy. Finally, we have the **promotors** and the hope is that most of your customers are normally within this group.

The calculation for NPS ignores the passives and is calculated as the percentage of **promoters** minus the percentage of **detractors**.

As an example, with 20% detractors, 30% passives and 50% promotors, your NPS score would be calculated as 50% minus 20% = 30. Although we would all love a score of 100, anywhere up from a score of 30 is often considered acceptable.

2. The Next Step

With regular transactional feedback coming in from your clients don't ever forget to be grateful to your customers for them giving you this feedback. Often, I speak with coaching clients who have a process to react to negative feedback but do nothing with positive feedback. Your process here should include both.

Negative or neutral feedback should gain a rapid response from you. If there is something you can do to put right the issues the customer is flagging to you, you should do it. A customer with a service issue that gets resolved quickly and to their satisfaction is often one of your future most loyal customers.

Positive feedback although less critical from a timing point of view also requires some action on your behalf to acknowledge receipt. What is important here is showing gratitude for all the feedback customers spend their time and effort to send you. This needs to be in an authentic way.

An automatic email response to say, "thanks for the feedback", doesn't cut it here. Depending on your sector and volume of customers, an occasional gift would probably be received more warmly. A tub of chocolates or a tray of cupcakes to say thank you, which in turn so often leads to amazing positivity on social media too.

3. Business Improvement

Any process for measuring customer satisfaction at its heart needs to be about business improvement. Of course, by this stage, you will have dealt with your customer's current issues, but what you haven't yet done is stopped those issues from recurring in future. How could you have avoided causing customer dissatisfaction?

At Step 2 you can only react. The customer tells you it's not all okay and you need to react quickly to resolve their issues the best you can. This step however is more about a measured response. To achieve that we need to review the feedback data in aggregate looking for recurring issues and trends.

Every time you receive feedback from customers categorise meaningfully why you believe they gave that feedback. If your customer feedback mechanism allows customers to add some words to their choice of mood face, your job is almost done.

Typically feedback for most sectors split into speed, quality of service, communication and maybe value for money. Interestingly, all four of those crop up as things that make people either happy or sad. What you learn will also feed into your **Delivery - Root Cause Analysis** process from the last chapter.

If your customers are collectively telling you that your communication is not great, maybe you should consider finding ways to improve your communication. If your customers are collectively telling you they love your speed of service, maybe you should ensure all customers receive that same speed of service.

Importantly, looking at the aggregate data at this stage stops you from reacting (or more likely taking it personally and over-reacting) to one individual 'complaint' about your business.

4. Closing the Loop and Social Proof

The biggest complaint I hear from customers is "Well, I give feedback but nothing changes so what's the point?".

To avoid this, step 4 is to make sure you provide some feedback to your customers to show you are listening. If you make changes, communicate this. It could be directed back to your customers or via your social media channels. This openness will help you gain more feedback, allowing you to make further improvements to your customer's perception of your business.

If you get enough customer satisfaction data coming in you can use it as one of the metrics that you can base your employee performance rewards upon.

It is worth encouraging your team to request feedback from customers. Of course, they will be tempted to only ask customers who they know received their best efforts, but by talking about the mechanism, the customers will also remember to use it when they were served less well.

Finance - Budget

The Why?

I think people don't like creating budgets, because they are often made too complicated, laborious to create and difficult to see the value of doing them. In my youth, the only reason I would put together a business plan, budget and cash flow forecast was for the bank as part of a finance application. Of course, I wanted those guys to see me in the best light so I probably didn't outright lie, but certainly gave them a flowery spin on my reality.

Where budgets are produced, they are often not shared with the team but put on a shelf and allowed to gather dust. This is not unusual, especially if you don't understand how to use it to inform your business decisions.

In summary, why budgets often don't work.

- They are not truthful.
- They are not shared with the business stakeholders.
- Decisions are not being made based on the data.

Working through this section, you will create a budget that will become one of your best indicators of current health and future business direction.

The topics covered include:

- The importance of the truth.
- The numbers you should include in your budget.
- Budget vs Cash flow forecast
- Creation, review and reset cadence.
- Variance and Influencing Decision Making.
- Deciding who should see the budget and the need for training.

Method

The cut-and-thrust of the small business world often means that budgeting is not high up the priority list, but I want this chapter to change your view to make a budget the most logical tool to help you achieve financial success.

The importance of the truth

Don't lie to yourself when you create your budget.

The issue with any forecast such as an operating budget is that at its essence you will be guessing at some numbers. The chances of achieving your guessed number will be relative to the amount of truth that went into forming your educated guess.

As such, don't just assume you will double your turnover and half your costs in the next 12 months without some serious understanding of how likely that will happen.

The numbers you should include in your budget

If you have never produced an operating budget before, start simple with only a few headings and sub-headings. You can expand on these later, as your understanding of budgets increases and your need for a more detailed budget grows.

- **Total Revenue, including**
    1. Revenue from the sale of re-sold products and services
    2. Revenue from the sale of your labour services
- **Total Cost of Goods, including**
    3. Cost of products and services you resell.
    4. Cost of your labour for services you resell.
- **Gross Profit (Total Revenue minus Total Cost of Goods)**
- **Total Operating Costs, including**
    5. General Administration Costs
    6. Sales and Admin Labour costs
    7. Management Labour Costs
- **Net Profit (Gross Profit minus Operating Costs)**

As you can see from the list above, there are just seven figures you will be looking to put into your first budget. As per the above example, try and tie up the corresponding revenue to the cost of goods related to generating that revenue.

Budget vs Cash Flow Forecast

A cash flow forecast helps you understand the timing difference around the flow of money coming into your business and money being paid back out.

For example, if you pay £1,200 for an annual insurance policy in January, you need the money in the account to pay the bill, but from a budgeting point of view, this is a prepayment for a service that will be delivered across the year with a cost of £100 per month, or maybe £300 per quarter.

I am not saying cash flow is not important as it critically is, but this chapter is about budget setting and using that to influence your business decisions.

Creation, review and reset cadence

Operating budgets help businesses run on leading data, rather than trailing data. By this, I mean that without an operating budget, business owners are often dependant on waiting for their accountant to tell them how well they did in the previous year. This is much too late to create any change that will impact the year's outcomes.

So, for your first budget, consider creating a quarterly plan. Effectively four mini budgets next to each other adding up a complete year.

	Q1	Q2	Q3	Q4	Total
Sale of re-sold things and services					
Sale of your labour services					
Total Revenue					
Cost of things and services you resell.					
Cost of labour for services you resell.					
Total Cost of Goods					
Gross Profit (Total Revenue minus Total Cost of Goods)					
General Administration Costs					
Sales and Admin Labour Costs					
Management Labour Costs					
Total Operating Costs					
Net Profit (Gross Profit minus Operating Costs)					

Create a table like the one on the previous page and start by extracting from the last four quarters how your business achieved. This will help you see if there is a pattern and relationship between revenue, cost of goods, operating costs and of course your profits.

Where you can, align the sales and the cost of sales into the same quarter. And as mentioned previously, break the large costs for annual services into quarterly amounts that time in with when the service is delivered to you.

What can we learn from this step of the process?

Is there a noticeable difference between your best performing and worst-performing quarter? What causes this? Was it something in your control? Could you repeat the actions of the best performing quarter or perhaps ensure you don't repeat whatever caused your worst-performing quarter. If there is a marked difference between your best and worst quarter, consider repeating this exercise looking at the year prior, which will help you see if there is a trend.

The next step is to create your budget. Assuming you are not in a seasonal business, are you looking for regular growth across the year? Again, consider how much you grew last year against the prior year. Is this repeatable or desirable?

We have two income streams within my example. If you pick a 10% growth would that be the same for both income streams?

The cost of goods is likely to grow as a proportion of your income streams until you have a big enough business to have greater buying power.

Lastly, if you achieved 10% more sales revenue, what impact would that have on your operating costs. If you can work from the same office, with the same admin team and don't need to recruit new sales or management resources, hopefully, these costs will not increase by 10%.

Business operating success from a financial point of view is essentially creating a greater amount of gross profit pounds (even if it's at the same percentage) without the operating costs increasing at an even greater pace to swallow it all up, so you end up with a greater retained net profit.

Add a second set of columns to your table for actuals across the whole year and you now have your first operating quarterly budget. Look to have added your figures within a week of closing out your quarter to keep this document fresh and meaningful.

Variance and Influencing Decision Making

The differences, or variances, between your budget and actual, are important.

If revenue has slipped from what you budgeted to achieve, what is the impact of your budgeted operational costs. You can't spend it if you don't have it.

If revenue is massively more than you expected, again what is the impact on your operational costs. If you need more resources, knowing your sales revenue is up should help you decide to invest.

Your variance should be accrued across the year. If quarter one's sales didn't go to plan, what can you do in quarter two to get back on track?

Deciding who should see the budget and the need for training

The last point in this chapter is about who should get to see the budget within your business. My advice would be that the leadership team should have a full and detailed working understanding of the whole of the budget. They must know how their job impacts the ability of the business to deliver against the budget plans.

There are also some advantages of helping the wider team understand what you are looking to achieve but this is not without its risks. My advice here is to teach your team at a level they can easily understand, else access to the numbers will either bring false confidence or scare them!

Finance - Credit Terms

The Why?

The time between selling your products and services and getting paid for them is called debtor days. The smaller the number the better. A well-run business will typically have debtor days of less than 30. To calculate yours, use this formula.

Current Aged Debt / Annual Revenue * 365 = Debtor Days

As an example, let's assume you have annual revenue of £900K and at the end of any month, you are owed £120K the formula would look like this.

£120,000 / £900,000 * 365 = 48.6 days

If through reviewing and enhancing your credit control you could improve your cash flow and only have £60K owing to you at the end of each month, you will have created the following outcome.

£60,000 / £900,000 * 365 = 24.3 days

Some business sectors are notoriously slow at paying but they are typically also the businesses that have the most frequent instances of business failure. Their failure can cause your failure. No fault of yours, except for your decision to lend them too much of your money and for too long.

When a prospect advised me that they wanted a 90-day credit term, else they would not give me their business, I walked away. Not in the early days, but once I realised that I was not their financier.

Now what you are owed at the end of each month will include some potential for bad debt. You can't just exclude it but you do need to take some proactive decisions about collecting it, assuming it's collectable.

Remember, you didn't set out to be your customer's banker and whilst your money is sitting with them it's not enabling your success. That is unless your business is a bank!

Method

In 1996 I had the pleasure of working with a business consultant who spent what seemed like an inordinate amount of time drilling into me the concept of 'contract review'. It is mostly a discussion about risk, but the four high points of this topic from memory were to gain clarity of what we would be doing for the customer when we would be doing it, how much we were going to be paid and critically when we were going to be paid.

You would have thought with that education I would never lend my money badly, but over the years I have had many sleepless nights due to my poor judgement.

The relationship between debtor and creditor days

With your new knowledge of your debtor days, we can now look at your creditors.

Creditor days are the equivalent concerning the time it takes you to pay your suppliers. Take how much you have on credit at the end of the month and divide it by how much you buy on credit in the year and multiply it by 365.

If your debtor days (how long you lend money for) is greater than your creditor days (how long you borrow money for), you have a risk of running out of money even if on the face of it you have a good level of sales revenue. An overdraft may be a short-term fix, but ultimately you need your debtor days to be less than your creditor days

Elastic Credit Terms

If a customer asks for, or just takes, extended credit terms what does that tell you about their business operation? Often this kind of request comes with a tale of woe about how they are owed a lot of money from one of their biggest customers.

What they are telling you is that their debtor days (money their customers owe them) are negatively impacting their creditor days (the money they owe you). Instead of fixing the issue with their customers, they have decided to shift that problem to their suppliers (you) which is at best a short-term fix to their business challenges.

You should do what you can to resist this type of accidental increase in your credit terms. Remember, you are exposed to the total amount of their indebtedness to you. Would their business failure hurt your business? If so, you have a duty to your business and staff to not just extend your exposure without fully understanding the additional business risks.

Ideas for reducing debtor days

Existing customers may be tricky to change but all new customers don't know how generous your credit terms were. If you create a new policy that everyone pays for everything upfront before you deliver the service, I wager you would still be able to create a successful new business.

For my IT business, the game changer was moving to a direct debit scheme as the payment standard for both recurring invoices and one-off projects. If a customer refused to pay by direct debit that was normally a sign that at some point, they would become a bad debtor. This scheme put our business in control of the timing of collecting payments and of course, we were never exposed for more than a month of provided services.

For most businesses having debtor days of less than 30 and creditor days of greater than 30 is a great target to aim for. Knowing these figures and any trend in their changes are critical to the prudent financial management of your business.

Debt collecting options

Your money in your customer's hands is at risk. Until it is in your bank account you can't use it to fund your next project to make more money. If you can't get your customers over to a direct debit scheme, you could offer them a discount scheme for early settlement. Or in the case of old debts, a discount to collect as much of the money as you can.

If you know you will need to give a discount to collect your money, you will probably need to increase your prices to allow for this discount to be taken off. There are third-party companies that will handle the collection for you if you prefer called invoice factoring or invoice discounting companies but typically these do not remove the risk. Any bad debt will still be your problem.

Taking business that 'keeps the lights on'

When things are quiet for your business, it's tempting to take any order just to keep the wheels turning. Maybe work that is not as profitable as you normally like or even something you may do as a loss-maker given that you have already committed to some of your labour costs etc.

What I want you to do here is to consider when deciding to take this type of order to look at the payment terms closely. Imagine doing sub-economic work and then the customer taking a lifetime to pay you too.

Until you get your invested money back into your account you can't start on your next order, so knowing when you will get paid remains the most critical.

Credit ratings and debtor insurance

Time for a short story. Back in 2005, my company was providing services to a regional airport. My whole team loved the airport and the staff that worked there. It was a feather in our cap to be the chosen provider for all their computer-related needs. We had even developed software for their flight movements and display boards in the lounges. When the company failed, flights were cancelled and aeroplanes were grounded and we were left being owed about £30,000.

In the facilities team break room on the day of the collapse, I sat around with airport staff and contractors as we licked our collective wounds about the loss of livelihood and money. I got chatting with the supplier of their high voltage services who introduced me to the concept of debtor insurance and their £1,000,000 project to install some underground cabling. Essentially, before they started work, they sent the proposal to their insurer so they could confirm they would be good to cover the risk.

I said, "Oh, so you are laughing. Why are you here with us today?". The chap said, "Well, the insurer said that they wouldn't cover the risk but we chose to deliver the project anyway!".

The lesson here is, check the credit ratings of your customers and prospects and use that knowledge to inform your decision making. And if you use an insurance company to cover your risk from debtors, don't override their decisions.

Finance - Financial Control

The Why?

Let's start this chapter with the parallel of the control of your home finances.

When you have multiple wages coming into your home and life is good you probably don't look too closely at your regular subscriptions. Then a life-changing event happens, leading to you dropping to one income and that is the catalyst for you to review just where all your money goes.

That's the time you consider whether you watch enough on Netflix to keep the subscription etc. Until then, you could afford it so you didn't think about it.

Well, that same thing happens in business. You look at the profit at the bottom line, decide it is about right and never look any further until you suffer a business changing event such as losing a large customer or suffering a large bad debt.

The issue with this approach is typically anything going wrong will be a serious problem before you even know about it.

Having a plan to regularly review your business finances will allow you to remain proactive about improving your profitability, leading to sustainable business success.

The three areas you need to have a strategy for reviewing are:

- **Customers**
- **Products and Services**
- **Business Expenses**

Within your strategy you will also need to consider the cadence of your reviews and who would be the right stakeholders to help with this process.

It is possible to have an otherwise amazing business that still fails due to a lack of financial control. And of course, that outcome is avoidable.

Method

When you see someone in an art gallery stare at a painting for a while and then move to the other side of the room and stare at the same painting again. Generally, this is to get the sense of perspective that the artists wished to convey. It's amazing what you can learn by looking at it from another angle. From gaining another perspective.

The three areas we are going to discuss reviewing overlap. It could be that reviewing one area of the business brings you a fix to your current issues but stick at it and review all three areas. Your bottom line, annual shareholder dividend and ultimately business value will thank you for putting the effort in here.

1. Customers

Which of your customers are profitable today? Some may pay you a lot of money but use more than their share of your available resources. If that's true you may need to either increase the prices you charge them, become more efficient in what you do for them or replace them with customers who are more like your more profitable customers.

The first task here is to find out how profitable your customers are. Probably a chance to bring out your Microsoft Excel skills and create a spreadsheet. Depending on how good your record-keeping is, you may have to do some work to complete the details.

- **Step One** - Add up everything you have charged each of your customers in the last quarter. The total invoice value.

- **Step Two** – Deduct the cost of anything you have purchased to sell to the customer (normally called the cost of goods).

- **Step Three** – Deduct the labour cost for looking after the customer. This may be tricky, depending on how accurately you keep time records. The point is if junior staff have a cost of £10 per hour and senior staff a cost of £40 per hour, you need to know how much of each was needed to service the customer. Include costs for admin, quoting, customer service etc. All of those make up the cost of looking after this customer.

With this data collected, you can sort your customers based on profitability. What is the difference between the customers who contribute the most profit and those that don't? You may even learn that by the time you factor in your labour costs you have customers that you lose money to serve.

As a side effect of this process, you will also learn how much of your team's time is spent actively looking after customers. You may find you gain some efficiencies by just asking how their time is spent today.

If you have a time recording system, it should be possible to automate the creation of this report so on a monthly or quarterly basis you can review which of your customers need attention.

Non-Profitable Customers

Continue to service them and ultimately, your business will fail and you will run out of money. Look at the bottom 20% of your customers on the list and see if you can work out why they are not profitable. It will likely be one or both of these reasons.

- **You are not charging enough** – Put the prices up. Gently at first, especially if you haven't increased your prices in years. The worst case is that the customer who doesn't contribute to paying your bills leaves and you gain the additional capacity to find more profitable customers.

- **You are using too much time** – If a non-profitable customer is using more hours than you expect, is it something you can fix. Train your team and help them understand the time is money equation. Train your customer so they don't need as much of your team's time.

'Too Profitable' Customers

You are likely to find that if you have some customers who are generating more profit than is reasonable, it's only a matter of time before a competitor will lure them away and you will have no defence. If you wish to retain them in the longer term, be proactive about realigning their pricing to ensure you are fair.

From a stakeholder's point of view, the team must record their time accurately. Anyone working with customers in any capacity should understand why knowing if 'Customer A' or 'Customer B' requires more resource is important for the business rather than them left thinking that this is just about you checking up on them.

2. Products and Services

However simple your original model was when you started, over the years typically most businesses end up with a broad list of products and services being regularly sold. The question is, are the prices being charged correctly for what you are expecting the business to achieve?

There are many methods for creating selling prices that essentially split into two.

- **Cost-Plus** – This is where your selling price is based on knowing what it costs to deliver your service to which you then add your expected profit margin on top. If it costs £20 to deliver your service and you want to make a 20% profit, you will add £5 and sell at £25.

- **Value-Based** – This is where the price is set based on what the customer is willing to pay for the described benefits. As such, if your service is the best in the market your customer will pay you £30. Your cost is still £20 to deliver, so you will make £10 profit, 33%.

The main issue with value-based pricing is that if the customer only believes the benefits to be worth £15 and it costs you £20 to deliver it you will lose £5 every time you sell your service. It could be that you just have not explained the benefits well enough for the customer to understand and buy into the value you propose.

Next, let's work through recalculating selling prices for all your services, by following these steps for each of them.

1. **Step One - Cost Price** – Calculate the cost price. Include any raw material costs plus all labour required to sell, install, service and support your product.

2. **Step Two – Market Pricing** – Find out how much others sell comparable products. I have often heard the 'but we are unique so can't be price compared' argument, but typically the customer doesn't especially see you as unique. As such, compare yourselves to who you think your customers would compare you with.

3. **Step Three – Calculate your cost-plus price** – Take the cost price from Step One and add the margin you need to make. Remember, this is your gross margin ahead of any operational or office costs. From my IT business we worked on a 50% gross margin, so would multiply the cost price by two to arrive at a cost-plus selling price.

4. **Step Four – Calculate your value price** – From the market pricing you discovered, how much do you think you could charge for your version of the service. If it's going to be sold at more than the current market price, what messaging around your benefits do you think you could communicate within your sales activity?

If the **value-based** price calculated in step four is less than the **cost-plus** price calculated in step three you won't achieve the level of profit you require to reach your business goals.

- Review whether you can buy smarter to make this value-based price work and if you can't, you may want to reconsider selling this line.

- You may still choose to sell at this price as a 'loss leader' but be careful that unless you are selling enough profitable services a loss-leading service could cause you to become a loss-making business.

Now you have your new selling price for all new business, work out which of your customers currently buy this service at less than its price and create a strategy to bring them up to your new pricing. Else, you can consider helping your customers move to alternative services that you can deliver to them for their available budget.

I recommend you review all your products and services at least annually and from a stakeholder perspective, this is a project for the finance team initially and then the sales and account management team to help get the new pricing messages out, should you need to increase prices.

Business Expenses

As mentioned at the start of this chapter, typically business expenses are only given real attention when things are going badly. Up until then, they are considered to be fixed expenses.

You will be surprised how many are not fixed, but they will need your attention.

Start by listing everything you have purchased in the last year that wasn't factored in the products and services cost of goods work you completed in the last section.

You will have headlines such as office rental, utilities, insurance, phone lines, accountant, banking, IT support, waste handling and many others.

For each line, you need to ask the following three questions.

- **Use** - Is it still used? You may find phone lines that are no longer needed or software that is being paid on a recurring subscription that you have migrated away from.

- **Capacity** - Is there extra capacity that's not needed? Do you pay for a weekly waste collection when fortnightly may be OK? Are you renting offices that are too large?

- **Price** – So assuming you need to keep the service is the price you are paying fair or is there a discount to be requested from the supplier? Some industries such as insurance seem to habitually increase your rates until you query them, at which point they magically find you a loyalty discount. It's yours for the asking!

You can't save your way to long term business profitability

What I mean by this is that the first time you undertake this process you will likely make some substantial savings, maybe 10 to 20% off your regular business costs. You will become more profitable almost overnight.

However, when you revisit this in a year it may be harder to make the same level of additional savings. Especially if you and your team start becoming more sensitive to and resistant to taking on recurring costs and subscriptions. That said, an annual review is probably about right for this process.

Although again, this will be owned by the finance team it's great for the whole team to know that there is a focus on business costs. Invite suggestions of where the business can make savings and you may be surprised what they recommend.

34 Modules

Foundation Plan

Purpose, Vision & Mission	Core Values	Growth Plan	Medium Term Plan	Long Term Plan	Wider Perspective

Company

Organisational Chart	Corporate Image	Product & Service Offerings	Next Big Thing
Employee Wellbeing	Communication	Risk	Community

People

Leadership	Effective Meetings	Shining Stars	Holistic One-to-Ones
Pay Structure	Profit Sharing		Recruitment

Sales

Lead Generation	New Business Process	Pre-Sales Process	Proposals	Account Management	Pricing Strategy

Delivery

Project Management	Measurement	Root Cause Analysis	Customer Satisfaction

Finance

Budget	Credit Terms	Financial Control

Printed in Great Britain
by Amazon

63422324R00129